Citizens Gone Wild

Thinking for Yourself in an Age of Hype and Glory

George Zilbergeld

UNIVERSITY PRESS OF AMERICA, ® INC.
Lanham • Boulder • New York • Toronto • Plymouth, UK

Copyright © 2008 by
University Press of America,® Inc.
4501 Forbes Boulevard
Suite 200
Lanham, Maryland 20706
UPA Acquisitions Department (301) 459-3366

Estover Road
Plymouth PL6 7PY
United Kingdom

Library of Congress Control Number: 2008932644
ISBN-13: 978-0-7618-4131-9 (paperback : alk. paper)
ISBN-10: 0-7618-4131-8 (paperback : alk. paper)
eISBN-13: 978-0-7618-4213-2
eISBN-10: 0-7618-4213-6

For
Nancy, Ben, and Leah

Wisdom is a butterfly
And not a gloomy bird of prey.

—*W. B. Yeats*

Contents

Part I

WHAT EVERYONE "KNOWS"

The following questions are answered in this book. You probably already have at least an expectation about the answers, based on what you have learned through school, books, and the Internet and other mass media.

Check your assumptions now and read on to see if you know the *real* story. An answer key is provided in the appendix. Do the facts match what you would expect? If not, what caused you to make an incorrect assumption?

In a formal educational setting, students may answer the questions before reading this book, then answer the same questions and compare before-and-after responses. Students also can use the library and Internet to look for the answers, critiquing the level of bias encountered in sources, if you think there is any bias in the answers.

1. Between 2001 and 2003, ___ people in the U.S. died of diseases caused by the HIV-AIDS virus. During the same time period, ___ people in the U.S. died of cancer, and ___ people died of heart disease.
2. Each year, ___ U.S. police officers are killed in the line of duty.
3. ___ people are in the regular U.S. Army, Navy, Marines, Air Force and Coast Guard, not including reserve units.
4. Israelis have long debated a plan to give up the country's West Bank District for the establishment of a Palestinian nation. Without this land, Israel would be ___ miles wide at its "waist." (The waist is the narrowest width of the country.)
5. How long could the United States federal government operate on the incomes generated by those making at least $1 million a year if the government confiscated all of that income?

6. In 1989, the U.S. banned Alar, a chemical used to prevent apples from rotting prior to harvest, after tests on mice produced tumors. A child has to drink ___ quarts of apple juice to equal the level of exposure given to the mice.

7. According to the best documented and most comprehensive study on school performance, what two most important factors determine academic success?

8. In the year___ , Saudi Arabia outlawed slavery.
   In the year ___ , Mauritania outlawed slavery.

9. What are the world's five most deadly diseases?

10. During World War II, ___ were killed by the military forces of the Empire of Japan.
    During that same period, ___ Japanese were killed in hostile action.

11. Is average per capita household income highest among white, Asian, or black families?

12. The average per pupil expenditure in New Jersey is ___.
    New Jersey students ranked ___ among U.S. high school students in scores on the standardized Scholastic Aptitude Test (SAT).

13. The U.S. federal government of the United States spends ___ each day. How much is spent every hour?

14. The U.S. federal income tax burden paid by the wealthiest 1 percent of taxpayers is ___. The tax burden paid by the lower half of income earners is ___.

15. The land taken up by cities, highways, railroads, airports, and other development amounts to ___ percent of the total land mass of the United States?

16. The average American produces about four pounds of solid waste per day. Is this more or less than the average produced in 1900?

17. True or false: The average household in the U.S. produces one-third more garbage a day than the average household in Mexico City?

18. True or false: If all of the solid waste produced in the United States during the past century was placed in a landfill, that landfill would require less than 100 square miles (ten miles by ten miles).

19. ___ percent of all the paper used in the U.S. is produced from trees that are planted and grown for the apple industry.

20. Medical research grants are funded by the U.S. federal government according to mortality rate, so that the most money is spent on diseases causing the most deaths. This is why research dollars are spent on cancer (the primary cause of 650,000–750,000 deaths a year), rather than on preventing hang nails. The actual research dollars spent for some commonly discussed causes of death are:

___ for each lung cancer death.
___ for each prostate cancer death.
___ for each breast cancer death.
___ for each HIV-AIDS related death.

21. What are the ten most dangerous jobs in the U.S. in terms of the number of related deaths and injuries compared with the number of people employed?

Part II

TWELVE WAYS TO BECOME YOUR OWN PUBLIC POLICY EXPERT

Introduction: The Methods

I think that there should be a difference between someone who spends four years in a college and someone who spends four years in a bar.

The difference should be the ability to analyze public policy in a way that is more objective and sophisticated than what one would expect from a bar hound. This book, while useful in winning bar bets, is meant to do more. It is meant to provide everyone with the tools they need to make worthwhile judgments about public policy issues. If you are or were a college liberal arts major, these tools are particularly important, since they are methods with which you can think in a disciplined and objective manner associated with the natural sciences. I would also like to think that any citizen, regardless of educational level, can get some handy ideas in this book.

I have chosen these particular methods because they have wide application. In addition to helping you make objective public policy decisions, the methods are useful in many careers, and in the life of any active citizen. Once these methods become habitual they are powerful enough to be noticed and rewarded by colleagues, professors, supervisors, and fellow citizens.

It doesn't matter if you are tall or short, liberal or conservative, Democrat or Republican, black, white, or pinstriped—we all have our beliefs and ideas of how the world should and does work. Unfortunately, clear and disciplined analysis often destroys these ideas and brings a feeling of unease. Therefore, it takes a great deal of courage and discipline to question one's own beliefs.

Still, there is a certain pride that comes with the knowledge that you practice what you preach, when you preach about being open minded, and that you have the will to force yourself to question your own beliefs. It may help to keep in mind how much pain has been caused by people who refuse to rethink their views. Any increase in open-mindedness is a giant step forward. It may also help if we realize that people who appear frequently on television as experts rarely make predictions that are falsifiable and so rarely leave themselves open to challenge. I often wonder if these so-called authorities have much expertise beyond a celebrity's ability to get the word expert set alongside their names on the screen. The truth is that many public policy decisions would benefit from a healthy dose of common sense, and this book is just a way to encourage people to use common sense.

We often hold beliefs unsupported by reason, logic, and facts. Perhaps we believe things because everyone around us believes something to be true, or perhaps because we have been taught by schools, the government, or the media, to believe in a certain view of the world. Sometimes our beliefs are like old friends with whom we are reluctant to part, especially if they have often been there to comfort us.

It is easy to tell people to be open-minded, but it takes tremendous courage to actually be so. The goal of this book is to encourage you to do just that by teaching respect for the scientific attitude. This is an attitude of open-mindedness. Science operates to a large degree by presenting a view of the world, or part of it, and inviting anyone to examine this view and agree or disagree. Although most of the time the audience is one trained in the sciences it is this willingness to allow others to look and see for themselves that is the heart of the matter.

Although science is often identified with experiments made in the natural sciences such as biology and chemistry, science also occurs in areas where conducting an experiment is very difficult. The best example may be astronomy, where access to the heavens for experimentation is quite limited. The attitude of being open minded is one of the most important pillars of science. This does not mean that this method is pleasant for scientists. I imagine that very few scientists are pleased to be proven wrong. Still, if you want to call yourself a scientist you must give others the opportunity. I also think that if you want to call yourself an open minded citizen you need to adopt as much of an open minded attitude as you can.

Willingness to be proven wrong doesn't seem natural to me. I doubt if it comes naturally to anyone. I assume that being open-minded is a hard to acquire discipline that, like other disciplines, produces wonderful results, but is still hard each and every time it is applied.

The goal is to produce a specific model of how the world works, and then test this model using appropriate methods. The implicit premise is that you will be open-minded enough to accept a different finding and adjust your views. It was a bet of the Founding Fathers of this nation that we would produce enough citizens willing to do this in order to make this country work for centuries to come. This book does not focus so much on what your views are, but rather on how you hold your beliefs. Are you willing to modify or give them up if the evidence points you in a different direction?

In the social sciences we have trouble giving a definite answer to any question. We often can only accumulate evidence that supports or contradicts our hypothesis (model of the world). In analyzing situations we face as a citizen or at work, these methods will suffice to take our thinking well above the level of openness used by most students or citizens.

Chapter One

Facts

Mitch Snyder, a crusader for the homeless during the later part of the twentieth century, traveled throughout America bringing attention to the plight of the homeless. In frequent interviews for news stories, he often said that there were 2 million to 3 million homeless people in America. Sometimes, however, he used the figure of 6 million homeless.[1] During the last decade of the twentieth century, there were many local and national stories about the homeless on television and in print. Organizations were created to help those who slept on the street or in public bus stations or shelters.

Mitch's figure of millions of homeless seemed to be accepted by all; perhaps no one wanted to appear so callous as to ask to see the study that showed so many sleeping on the streets. When one study was done in Chicago by reputable researchers, it was found that there were only 13 percent as many homeless as the advocates for the homeless said. The result was that the research organization was attacked as heartless and mean spirited.

Eventually, a respected sociologist did a scientific study and found that the number of homeless in America was about three hundred thousand. He also found that, contrary to the television images of street children and families, 80 percent of the homeless were single men. Someone asked Mitch about the figure of several million homeless.[2] Mitch said that he had just made up the number to draw attention to the homeless.

After this news filtered out, there was a sharp decline in the number of stories on the homeless.[3] Action was still taken to help those who were homeless and more shelters opened, especially in the big cities, but reporters no longer spoke of millions of homeless people.

Perhaps what is remarkable about this story is that it is actually not all that remarkable. People often go along with the picture in their heads, including those whose job title of "reporter" or "professor," implies that they think before they talk. This is especially so if questioning the picture in their heads might cause pain. At any point in time, there is a definite and dominating opinion among elite opinion makers. It is very hard to oppose the elite with another position, without experiencing a good deal of pain. In the example of the homeless numbers, questioners faced the additional burden of being labeled "cold—heartless and rotten to the core."

I want you to feel at ease when checking to see if the "facts" are true. I think that looking for facts in support of an argument can be fun, but my wife says that I, as a professor, should not consider myself normal.

Considering some of my colleagues, I tend to agree. I can say with confidence that knowing facts can provide you with confidence in your views and can be used to win public arguments. Anyway, most of what you are being asked to do takes place in the privacy of your own mind. You can always decide that this is the place to keep your new views.

When collecting facts, read thoroughly. People do lie by abusing facts, relying on the fact that many Americans read by skimming the headlines. Here is a fact from USA Today: "8,000 Troops Desert During the Iraq War."[4] You might be pleased or displeased by this news. But before you do anything serious, read further. The overall desertion rate actually has dropped since the September 11, 2001, attacks. So why mention the Iraq war and the number of overall desertions in the same headlines? You will have to ask the fellow who wrote the headline. My guess is that he or she is against the war in Iraq.

Facts are the base upon which you should found your arguments. Facts can save your integrity by changing your mind before you start to construct your arguments.

Public policy discussions always get around to talking about the number of children in welfare families. If folks on welfare have a large number of children, then perhaps these families carry some blame for their plight. Before you take sides about whether to blame families on welfare for bearing a lot of children, see whether families on welfare actually do have a lot of children. Look it up.[5]

Since almost any fact can be independently located in five minutes using some readily available sources, I looked it up. It turns out that 71 percent of the families on welfare have one or two children, and 9.6 percent have four or more. Whatever the causes of being on welfare, family size doesn't seem to be a major factor.

Some have suggested that one way to lift people out of welfare is to raise the minimum wage. Others argue that raising the minimum wages hurts the poor because it reduces the jobs available to unskilled people. An employer might take a chance at a lower wage but not at a higher one.

Would it help to learn that in 2005 only 9 percent of those below the poverty line were adults working forty-hour weeks? How can we use this information from the U.S. Census Bureau? First, you might feel good that in America only 9 percent of those below the poverty line are adults working full time. You might also decide that this is a manageable number if you support policies designed to improve the lot of those in poverty; you only have to help 9 percent of the working population.

If raising the minimum wage would move more full-time workers above the poverty line it might be worth it, since those not getting a job would be children, and perhaps they do not need the money as much as adults.[6]

Is poverty a trapdoor or a revolving door? Do the poor in America stay poor, or is the situation often temporary? According to the study by the Census Bureau, 5.3 percent of the poor population lives below the poverty line for two years. About 13 percent have incomes within the poverty range for over two years.[7] It would seem that, for most people, poverty is a temporary situation. What is the most likely reason to be poor? A broken family. Female-headed families are more likely to be poor and to stay poor.[8] Knowing the facts might help in thinking clearly about solutions to poverty. One more fact is that the current minimum wage is $7.25 an hour. If both a husband and a wife work full time, they will earn two times the minimum wage or $14.50 an hour, before withholding.

Multiplying that by forty hours in a week brings income to $30,160 a year gross (before taxes and other withholding). That is considerably above the poverty level of $20,650 a year for a family of four (U.S. Department of Health and Human Services guidelines for 2007, excluding Hawaii and the District of Columbia). Remember that $7.25 is only the bottom minimum wage. Many states mandate a higher minimum. This information was found simply by typing the words "U.S. poverty guidelines 2007" into a search engine, which gave not only the HHS guidelines but guidelines for every other government assistance program.[9] There is no single poverty guideline, but the Health and Human Services numbers are those usually considered. Do this a few times, and the practice of looking for facts becomes habitual.

Before the politically correct had such a massive effect on college campuses, talking after you looked up the facts was taught as the proper procedure. An educated person was expected to behave this way. They might not do so but they were expected to try and be embarrassed when someone said they were not doing so. At the very least, one was expected to have some respect for trustworthy people and sources that actually did have a command of the relevant facts.

After the advent of political correctness, the better part of valor, at least on some college campuses, has been to get the correct view first, and then either look for backup data, or just keep quiet until you have graduated and married well. Some think that since the 1980s, the left has made universities into a kind of church where facts are only respected if they support the catechism of the politically correct. At too many universities it has even become acceptable to shout down or slander anyone who deviates from the currently acceptable view of the world. The point is that you need to be careful out there if you are on a college campus. I don't want a student to be too bold, leave college and have to come and live at my house.

The joy and necessity of recycling has become an accepted truth. According to Martin Gross, who questions the usual line of reasoning, household recycling is usually not worth nearly the amount of money it costs. Gross found that consumer-driven recycling is virtually worthless, and most garbage is created by industry anyway. Business-created garbage amounts to over 7 billion tons a year, while consumer trash piles up to around 116 million tons. Industrial recycling deals in such massive quantities that there are efficient recycling methods, and the industries usually make more than they spend to handle garbage. So self-interest takes care of most of the recycling need. Consumer recycling is not economical because the pickup and sorting costs are too high and the income from selling paper and plastic is too low. Hardly anyone wants to buy old newspapers.[10]

It takes discipline to look for facts, remembering those pictures already in our heads that fit our worldview. We can claim busyness when it comes time to give our ideas a reality check; more truthfully, we might be wrong and have to go against "what everybody knows." Looking for facts can be painful. So without strong habits, the easier path is to protect our view of the world. But you could forge a new identity based on your open-mindedness, and this might be good fun as well.

There is another reason why it is hard to discipline yourself to fact find on your own. A fair amount of the time, the facts you find will counter what mainstream media is reporting. Even if we are independent and open-minded thinkers, it is extremely hard to go against the current media view of what to think and what to think about.

The media are usually obsessed with threats to health. Based on what you have heard, list the diseases you think will kill the most people worldwide in a typical year. We will look at the top nine. If you have taken the quiz in Part 1, you already know part of the answer. Table 1.1 lists the totals from the World Health Organization, which is considered the gold standard in this area of public policy relating to health.[11]

I doubt if anyone who is not a professor specializing in this area would identify and group the leading killers in this order. There are great differences from the perceptions one would get by reading in the Humanities and the Social Sci-

Table 1.1.   Leading Causes of Death Worldwide

Cause of Death	Deaths per Year
1. heart disease	7.2 million
2. vascular disease	5.5 million
3. respiratory infection	3.9 million
4. HIV/AIDS	2.8 million
5. pulmonary disease	2.7 million
6. prenatal complications	2.5 million
7. diarrhea-related diseases	1.8 million
8. tuberculosis	1.6 million
9. malaria	1.3 million

ences. The American media doesn't talk much about many of the above diseases because they are of little interest to Americans, who live in a country where many of these diseases are better controlled and more treatable.

Most people are mainly interested in what affects them. While that is only human, an educated person is compelled to heed the facts. For those in government or Non Governmental Organizations (NGOs), operating in accord with the facts can have vast implications when it comes to efficient spending that benefits those who need help. Knowing the facts can affect our policy choices as citizens who can get involved and at least vote. In relation to the above diseases, every citizen has some influence about how money is spent in medicine and medical aid with the intent to save lives.

For example, on the above list of diseases, some can be bunched as dirty water and dirty air diseases. In a certain sense, this is good news.

It isn't too expensive to reduce the prevalence of diseases such as malaria by perhaps 90 percent. Unfortunately one of the most important components is not politically correct: The use of DDT to destroy mosquito breeding grounds in stagnant water was one of the most important steps taken to eradicate malaria as a major threat in Western nations. We know it works because about one hundred years ago we used it to eliminate most cases of malaria in Europe and North America. That's a reason to read history, as we will see below. We could save the overwhelming majority of the 1.3 million lives lost in a year. DDT is cheap, and many people in the poor countries would be pleased to be paid to do the work, supporting their families while saving their families from malaria.[12] For many years, since Silent Spring was published by one of the first environmentalists, DDT has been a politically incorrect solution to this problem.

Facts matter, and in this case, facts can save lives. Ideology can kill.

A good deal of the developing world's water can be made safe by using inexpensive chemicals at easily constructed central water treatment plants. Doing this would reduce those falling ill because of dirty air and water diseases and would also sharply reduce diseases in the "diarrhea" category. These diseases do not cause the relatively mild diarrhea that you may have endured for one or two days. The kind of diarrhea that kills involves rapid and massive loss of fluids. It has killed tough soldiers over the centuries and certainly kills the weak. Chemicals such as chlorine that are inexpensive and easy to make, are wonderful friends of humankind.[13]

Dirty air is another problem in poor nations and kills millions in poor countries. We are talking about very dirty air that must be breathed all the time, not just the kind of dirty air that causes an air quality alert in cities a few days of the year. One dangerous source is the materials used to provide heat and fuel for cooking. Much of the world uses dung for fires. This sends large particles into the air to be inhaled into the lungs, killing millions. In the long run, when a country increases its wealth, safer fuels soon replace large particulate forming dung and firewood.

If you think it immoral to allow such easily preventable deaths to occur over much of the planet, then the compassionate policy might be for Western nations to build large central energy producing plants, just as we do in the United States. This produces the needed power without the harmful pollutants. We have the technology to avoid the air polluting generating stations that were once common.[14]

Putting all of this together, you might come to the conclusion that global thinking and action begins with enabling developing nations to build the treatment and generating plants we enjoy in the West.

We also have the means to reduce other third world problems, some of which have become first world problems with the increase in immigration. Tuberculosis can easily be controlled by isolating the contagious and ensuring that they take the proper medicine for about one year. This is exactly what occurred in the United States many years ago. One can still see large buildings that once were treatment centers for quarantined TB patients. You might consider whether isolation is better than death for the infected and their loved ones.

There is one great source that contains more relevant statistics on the United States than any other. This book, available in the libraries and now on the internet, is *The Statistical Abstract of the United States.*[15] It is useful for professors, students, professionals, and citizens generally and is a primary source for the television evening news and news shows.

Another easy way to find facts is to use an almanac. How much do we spend on food stamps? You can find the answer in less than one minute by looking in an almanac. How much do we spend on the military? You can find the answer in a matter of minutes by looking in an almanac.

The elderly often complain about the government. How much do we spend on them? Are the complaints warranted? According to Department of the Treasury statistics found in an almanac, only four items in the federal budget always cost over $100 billion a year. One is the defense budget, another pays for medical care for the poor, and the other two are for the elderly. You can agree or disagree if the United States spends enough on the elderly, but work with facts in framing an argument.

To most people in a scientific era, facts matter. They matter in college, in your career, and in your life as a citizen.

Some people say we spend too much on foreign aid and that we should take care of our own first. Many people have the idea that we could solve many budget problems if we just used foreign aid money in this country. How much do we spend on foreign aid? You can find out in less than a minute in an almanac. It will be about $17 billion. Is this more or less than you expected?

Did you check to see if I am telling the truth?

Statistical studies are available on an amazing number of topics, and many results end up in the Statistical Abstract. While it is true that statistics can be used to lie, it is also true that they can be used to encourage people to rethink their ideas.

Among arguments about the homeless, the question is asked whether their circumstances are the fault of society, unavoidable individual misfortune, or flaws in individual character. Facts might not settle the issue, but it is incumbent upon educated people to use facts. A recent study of homeless in city shelters found that 60 percent of the singles in the study abused alcohol and other drugs, and 30 percent of the adults in families in the city shelters abused alcohol or other drugs.[16] These numbers will not answer public policy questions regarding what should be done. They do elevate the argument to an appropriate level for educated adults. Most people would agree that to discuss policy regarding the homeless without mentioning these facts would be wrong. Such facts should be considered in determining policy.

Health care is a hot political topic in recent political campaigns. One reason people give for supporting universal health insurance is that we must help families avoid financial disaster. You can jump right in and argue with great passion, or you can act like a rational citizen and ask such questions as, "What portion of bankruptcy filings relate to health care costs?" For the year I checked, the Harvard Medical School Web site and the journal *Health Affairs* reports that medical costs play a significant role in about half of personal bankruptcies.[17] This doesn't settle the issue of what to do, but it does mean that any solution you propose will be based on facts and not just emotions. This habit of relying on facts will astound your teachers and peers while greatly annoying your opponents.

Public welfare is another topic that has stirred up emotions in recent years. When a lot of people think of welfare recipients, they imagine a mother surrounded by children. In fact, the number of children in families on welfare is about the same as the number of children in families that are not on welfare.

Do we want to increase or decrease the numbers of immigrants coming to this country? How many legal immigrants come into the U.S. each year? Shouldn't you know before you decide what your position is on immigration?

Should our social service agencies target special help on a particular racial group? The first thought is to suppose that a disproportionately high number of black families are in poverty. But should we find the relative incidence?

First write down your estimates for the following:

•White families in poverty: _____ percent.
•Black families in poverty: _____ percent.

Now look up the actual percentages in The Statistical Abstract.[18]

•White families in poverty: _____ percent.
•Black families in poverty: _____ percent.

Perhaps now you can see one reason none of us are totally at ease with facts. Facts often disturb our favorite beliefs. Most of our views of how the world works have been with us for a long time. They are friends who live in a back room of our head, available whenever we wish to chat. Facts, on the other hand, can be very annoying. Facts need to be checked because common sense isn't common and is often inadequate. Real life often contradicts our favorite beliefs; conditions change.

Another fact source is your Internet search engine. For example, "Google" the following stories:

"Tighter Border Yields Odd Result: More Illegals Stay."

"The very rich . . . give their share and even more."

"Doctors in financial difficulty?"

Be careful what you wish for when you say "Tax the rich." According to Internal Revenue Service information, available on the irs.gov Web site, in 2006 you needed to earn $328,000 per year to get into the top 1 percent bracket. To be in the top 5 percent, you needed to earn $137,000, and to get into the top 10 percent bracket you needed to earn $99,000 per year.[19] Do you think you and your spouse will earn enough to get into the top 10 percent of earners? Do you think that you and your spouse will be in the top 1 percent or 5 percent of income earners? Are you among the "rich?"

Are the rich paying their fair share? Look up the Internet-available facts: The top 1 percent pay about 37 percent of the federal income taxes. The top 5 percent pay 57 percent. The top 50 percent pay 96.7 percent of federal income taxes. That means the bottom 50 percent pay 3.3 percent of all federal income taxes. About one-third of tax filers do not pay one penny. This is why you can't give the poor a federal tax reduction. They don't pay federal income taxes. In fact, many low-income earners get money back, even though they don't pay anything. They have a negative tax burden, and receive money back through a program called the Earned Income Tax Credit.

Let us say that you worry that some people (probably a member of a group other than your own) are having too many children, and they could take over . . . what? Well, who knows? But they could take over, and once it is taken over you will miss it, whatever it is. You could look at the "Birth Rates" chart in the *World Almanac.*

By the way, if someone says at this point, "The almanac—who cares what they say?" you can explain that the *World Almanac* gets this birth data from the National Center for Health Statistics. Every Almanac I know of gets its data from reliable sources. Don't worry if you can't remember the exact title. Your opponents won't remember either. The point is to see that, from 1950 to 2002, the birth rate (births per thousand people) has gone from 24.1 to 14.5. Why do many people refuse to have more than two children? As people become educated and make a few bucks, their love of children wanes. Best of all, when people become educated, they are able to articulate good reasons for having fewer children. Thus, instead of saying, "I am exhausted day and night," they say:

- "I want to give my child the very best and everything is so expensive these days."
- "I would have more children, but I want to save the world and its resources."
- "Who can have children in such a terrible world?" (This one became popular after a 1960s survey quoted girls of Mills College in California.)

Historically, when people came to the U.S., they had a lot of children. They did not have access to birth control. They needed help on the farm. They needed someone to take care of them when they grew old. If you are afraid that one of these immigrant groups will take over, do a few minutes of research. You will learn that, after an immigrant group has been around for awhile, the high birth rate plummets. Few groups, if any, have a lot of children once they reach middle class status.

From time to time you will hear about how dangerous the world is. The local news will have headlines like "Carpets Kill." The intellectuals will say or imply that the water, the air, or other aspects of the environment are deteriorating because the government is being taken over by the rich and terrible, who only care whether we live or die if they make their fortune selling caskets.

Why not look and see how long people live? Look again at the *World Almanac*. If you are looking at "U.S. Life Expectancy at Selected Ages," you learn that in 1900 the life expectancy was 49.24 years and in 2002 it was 77.4 years. You would have to conclude that we are living longer and that this is partly because the environment and our medicine are better. Careful research shows that the air and water are much cleaner and safer today than in the past.

As an aside, let me suggest another source worth having on hand relating to these topics. If you want to look at charts that prove things are getting better in areas such as health, wealth, the state of poor Americans, housing, safety, environmental protection, natural resources, social indicators, women's rights, racial equality, and freedom and democracy, see *It's Getting Better All the Time: 100 Greatest Trends of the Last 100 Years* by Stephen Moore.[20] This book has information piled up in one spot.

Your teachers may have been telling you that the cause of HIV infection is unsafe sex, but you think that seems vague. It would seem that if you really wanted to save lives you would be a little more precise. Take a look in the Statistical Abstract chart "New AIDS Cases in the U.S., 1985–2002 by Transmission Category."

You will see that:

- Men who have sex with men comprise 55 percent of new HIV/AIDS cases.
- Intravenous drug users are 22 percent.
- Men who have sex with men and are also intravenous drug abusers add another 8 percent.

That leaves 15 percent for heterosexual sex and all other sources of infection.

In Africa, where HIV-AIDS infection has reached pandemic rates in some countries, other transmission factors are involved. Those who do not take part in high-risk behavior are far more likely to be infected by interpersonal contact.

Most people have busy lives and so, when they hear that some wilderness area is in danger of being developed or the president won't provide money to buy a forest to keep it in the public realm, they think Mother Earth is a goner. Yet, in the U.S., the public owns one third of the nation's land. Maybe this is not enough. You still have the final decision, but it will be a reasoned one if you find the facts.

There are facts that suggest that the liberal folks really do control most television news.[21] Liberals are people who want more government action on a variety of areas and this can sometimes result in certain facts are being mentioned as often as might be fair to a clear picture of reality. You don't have to go along with this view but you might want to be aware of it.

Frequently this viewpoint translates into a steady stream of public health scares. You may want to know whether you should gear up for this crisis or save your energy for the next one. A book by Adam J. Lieberman, Simona Kwan, and other contributors that will help: *Fact Versus Fears: A Review of the Greatest Unfounded Health Scares of Recent Times.*[22] Here you will learn a rule of thumb: It is the dose that makes the poison. This is the rule that scientists use. Remember that the next time television screams out that apples, hair dyes, coffee, men in latex, or whatever else, is killing us.

Hair dye caused cancer in rats. Rats usually do not care that much about their appearance, so they had to be forced to drink the dye. If this information is extrapolated to humans, one learns that you are in danger of getting cancer if you drink twenty-five bottles of dye a day. While rats really should do something about their appearance, most would not care to drink that much dye on their own. Most human beings are also too smart to drink twenty-five bottles of dye a day.[23]

The actress and part-time toxicologist, Meryl Streep, joined a group called Mothers and Others for Pesticide Control. They said that the chemical ALAR (generic name daminozide), a pesticide used on apples, causes cancer. It is true that daminozide causes cancer—if you were thirsty enough to drink nineteen thousand quarts of apple juice a day. Do yourself a favor and call a therapist if you feel compelled to drink even a hundred quarts of apple juice a day. Don't wait until you have a nineteen thousand-quart habit.[24]

Sometimes facts go against common sense. We have tightened our borders since the September 11, 2001, terrorist attacks. Whether we have tightened them enough is another question entirely. The fact that goes against sense is that tighter borders do not help keep illegal aliens out. Tighter borders result in more illegals staying once they are in the U.S., because if they go home they might not be able to get back. Much of the back-and-forth of people who came in from Mexico has turned into more forth and less back. The rational thing for an illegal immigrant to do under conditions of tight security is to become a permanent U.S. resident.

This kind of thing is so common that it has a name: *counter-intuitive.* While the facts may not lie, they do sometimes surprise us.

For years the media has been bombarding us with the news that women are paid less than men. Most people have just nodded and said that it must be true. Some who do not go along are intimidated by the feminists and have just stayed quiet. Actually, silence is a good choice if you are in public life or academia, where free speech is lauded in lecture but not practiced as often as we might wish.

In the past, there was a limited validity to this statement. The figure given in the past few decades was something like "Women are paid sixty-nine cents for every dollar a man is paid." You don't see that particular figure any longer. It has become so obviously false that even the more intense feminists got embarrassed and stopped using it.

If you compare all women and all men there is a discrepancy, but if you compare women and men with similar credentials and the same continuous work experience, the difference is minimal, no more than 5 percent of the total pay. A five-cent discrepancy is not good, but it is not thirty-one cents. Other numbers have been used recently. I recently heard use a new figure of seventy-six cents.[25] Wage disparity may not be as common as it used to be because gender discrimination is often not worth the economic risk. The government is watching, and the consequences of discriminating against women today can, and should be, costly.

The most important factor turns out to be continuous work experience. Women take off time to bear and raise children. Perhaps men should raise children, or government officials should raise them, or they should be taught to live off the land. But none of this changes the fact. Discrimination against women in today's work place is rare. You can check this out with Jane Waldfogel, a professor of Social Work at Columbia University, who says that young American women without children earn 95 percent of men's pay, while those with children earn 75 percent of men's pay.[26] Those with children earn less because they have interrupted a career to have children. You can say that men could have children if they only tried. What you cannot say with fidelity to the facts is that lower pay for women has much to do with discrimination. The evidence is clear. Generally speaking, gender discrimination is nowhere near as prevalent as it used to be. And there are many places, such as universities, where it is a decided advantage to be a women. Of course, if you want to keep saying something, you could say that it is society's fault for not providing everything from daycare, to public wombs, to keep women at work. Or, you can always just ignore the facts. This is best done if you have tenure.

Facts have a frumpy reputation. But sometimes they can be very sexy. Facts can be used to devastate your opponents' argument. There are facts that an ordinary ninety-pound citizen can use to stun a politician, or at least cause pause and puzzlement.

By the way, in 2004 the Immigration and Naturalization Service (INS) authorities issued penalty notices to three companies.

Those who are for letting the illegal immigrants stay here can make a powerful humanitarian argument. However, they are not satisfied with that and construct a more powerful argument by saying, "We have spent billions of dollars on border patrol agents and fencing. It hasn't helped at all." Such claims make me think that the people who say things like this are contemptuous of the average citizen.

Here are some facts to consider in an article in *The New York Times* by Eduardo Porter.[27] While we have spent a good deal of money to hire border agents, Porter shows that the border agents may not have the effect many people thought they would have. Only 4 percent of the agents enforce the law that says you can't work in the U.S. if you are here illegally.

This is less than half of the percentage assigned to enforce the law at the workplace in 1999. This is why the hiring of more INS agents will not really matter. It is as if you said you were hiring more Marines to shore up the nation's security but only 4 percent of the Marines were in units that had guns, while 96 percent of the Marines were sent to work in ice cream factories turning out more rocky road ice cream.[28]

Do you think we could stop more illegal immigration if we issued penalty notices to more than three companies in a year? The INS has almost completely stopped looking for illegal immigrant workers in the place where they are most likely to be found—the workplace. From time to time they start again, but during the last twenty years there has not been a continuous, serious effort to look for illegal aliens where they work. There may be a few well publicized exceptions but the rule remains.

While there is a law that says employees can only hire people who are here legally, the law doesn't provide a way that the employer can ensure compliance and assiduously avoids doing so. That means the employer can avoid paying a fine for hiring illegal employees by claiming ignorance. We have the beginnings of a program that would allow an employer to check to see whether an applicant is in the country legally, but it is voluntary, not mandatory, and not very good. A thorough database is at this moment being debated.[29]

Here is a powerful fact you might use if you are angry at rich people who don't seem to be working hard enough to earn the income they are receiving: Henry A. McKinnell, received $65 million in salary, stock, bonus, restricted stock, and incentive pay, while his company's stock lost 43 percent of its share value. This comes from Gretchen Morgenson, who writes for *The New York Times*. The title of this article is "Fund Manager, It's Time to Pick a Side."[30] McKinnell was Pfizer, Inc.'s chief executive officer and chairman of the board from 1999 to 2006. His golden payday for committing colossal bad management will stun those who say there is no need for government regulation of big business. Most of us have a selection of idiot relatives who would be willing to drive a company into the ground for a lot less.

Yet another fact with power: An estimated $92 billion a year is paid out in corporate welfare subsidies. This is according to the Cato Institute, a highly respected research organization.[31] If you want to argue for medical insurance for everyone, and people say it is too expensive, you can tell them about the annual bailout.

One problem with the mainstream media is that a good deal of their reportage is factual, but inane and misleading. After recent fluctuations in gasoline prices, there was a spate of stories on alternative sources of fuel for automobiles. Many concentrated on ethanol as an alternative fuel. All the ones I saw were misleading to one degree or another. All of the stories had that "Gee whiz, we have the answer, and the fools in Washington just won't listen to us" tone.

The 2005 statistic that we are already using over 4 billion gallons of ethanol a year sounds impressive. But it turns out that we use an average of 116 billion gallons of fuel each year. To go from 4 billion gallons to 116 billion gallons would require rebuilding the entire petroleum industry from scratch. These statistics are from the Energy Information Administration, Department of Energy.[32]

Television journalism does this all the time. Reporters often use whatever facts make them look wise and good. The saying, "If it looks too good to be true . . . ." is probably relevant here. There are numerous problems with ethanol, such as the fact that two-thirds of a gallon of another fuel like oil is needed to produce a gallon of ethanol, unless you want to pull the continental U.S. into a more Southern climate where you can grow immense quantities of sugarcane for ethanol.

Often the most effective use of facts is just not to mention them. Part of the liberal worldview is that immigrants are good, and this includes illegal immigrants. In all the articles on Lee Boyd Malvo (when he was convicted of the sniper murders of six people in the Virginia area in 2002), very few reported the detail that Malvo was an immigrant in the country illegally. He and his mother were found by the authorities and told to leave. Oddly enough they ignored the instructions to do that, as do many others. No one followed up.[33]

Facts in context issues often come up in connection with gun control. This is an area where there is a constant and dogmatic lack of facts. Sometimes, not reporting the stories is what skews the facts. There have been many stories about deaths caused by the misuse of guns. The reports often end with reinforcement of the position that we should ban or reduce gun ownership. Seldom seen are stories on incidents in which a gun saves a person or family from harm. Thousands of stories are available each year, such as one in a 2004 Houston, Texas, *Chronicle* I happened to see: "Homeowner shoots, kills intruder in Aldine." Such a story will seldom be picked up by the mainstream media, even though in this case the man who protected himself was seventy-nine years old.[34] Ideology often trumps thinking. The prevailing ideology of most reporters is anti gun. Their attitude is that this is their story and they are sticking to it.

Chapter Two

Comparative Analysis

Comparative analysis forces you to test how the real world matches the world of ideas in your head. Comparative analysis doesn't always give scientific proof or answer all questions, but it often is powerful enough to cause a reasonable and open-minded person to rethink issues. Ideological thinkers may experience extreme pain and prolonged periods of disorientation when faced with the results of analysis. Like hot sauce made in foreign lands, use with caution. It provides an important tool that can be used by anyone. It is quick, easy, and powerful.

Comparative analysis involves two steps:

1. Develop a hypothesis. A hypothesis is a theory that we use as a basis for further investigation. It is a model of how the world works that we submit to testing. It is an open-minded view that we have courage to change if we are good citizens.
2. Test the hypothesis across time and space. We ask if our hypothesis is true across time and space. Was our hypothesis true in the past? Is our model true anywhere we take it?

The law of gravity is a scientific law that explains things in the physical world. Laws of nature like gravity are more certain than laws in the world of social science and public policy. We cannot expect to achieve the same level of certainty in the social sciences as in the natural sciences, but we can pile up evidence that either supports or calls into question our views.

We need to force ourselves to test our assumptions. Methods such as comparative analysis never provide the certainty available with the law of gravity, but it can help us examine our fundamental ideas. When we consider how

much pain has been caused by people who refuse to rethink their views, we
will realize that even a modest gain of open-mindedness is a giant step forward.

Let us look at some examples of how we might use the concept of comparative analysis to test some of the theories we have sitting around in our
head, drinking lemonade and smiling.

We read in the paper that there is a lot of crime in Detroit and New York
City, so we develop the hypothesis that crowding causes crime. Perhaps we
think people get frustrated in crowded places and we decide that the denser
the population , the more crime a place will have.

Test this idea across time. It may seem that crowded areas such as cities
have a higher crime rate than non-urban areas. But we must test this hypothesis across space and here we see that very crowded countries such of England, Japan and the Netherlands have much lower rates of crime than cities in
the United States. Many foreign cities such as Tokyo also have a low rate of
crime.

The evidence indicates that dense population by itself doesn't seem to be
the key factor in crime. We have piled up enough evidence to convince us to
at least re-examine our view of how the world works.

Often in social sciences this is the best we can do. It is worth doing because it makes us examine our assumptions, and take another look at what
"everyone knows." In the social sciences we have trouble giving a definite
answer. We can only accumulate evidence that supports our hypothesis or
reduces support for our hypothesis. In most applications as a citizen or
when analyzing problems at work, this will be sufficient and well above
the level of openness and thoughtfulness used by most other students and
citizens.

Government spending is a topic that excites many taxpayers and we might
form the following hypothesis about it:

A. Hypothesis: Government spending hurts the economy. The more government spending we have, the less healthy and efficient the economy will
   be.
B. Look at governments across time and space.
   1. Time. If we look at Germany during the first three decades after World
      War II, when it recovered from devastation to become the strongest
      economy in Europe up to that point, we find that the spending of its
      central government was the highest in Europe. This would seem to say
      that you can have the government play an important role and still have
      a strong economy. The evidence is not definitive but it should be taken

into account. So far we may be uncertain as to what conclusion we might draw.

2. Space. The U.S. has a relatively small government sector compared with the countries of Western Europe, and we are currently very prosperous compared to Europe. But Japan has an even smaller government sector, and it holds the record for the most years of continuous growth among all nations, according to a 2005 report of the Institute of East Asian Studies of the University of California, Berkeley.
3. Time and Space. Countries with total control over the economy, such as communist countries of the past and present, have poorly functioning economies.

Perhaps our conclusion might be that the role of government in the economy is complex and hard to reduce to clear causes and effects. We do know that economies totally controlled by the government do poorly. We do not know the exact percent or the exact role that government should play in the economy to make it prosperous. The evidence we do have may make us reluctant to form firm judgments, and this might prevent us from making and defending dogmatic statements that are not so dogmatically true in the real world.

Politicians running for office usually say they wish to do something to both help people meet their medical needs while controlling costs. Many people think that socialized medical care, where the government provides or pays for medical care for everyone and decides on the correct price for services, will result in ever increasing costs and worse health care. It should not take long to see to see if this is true. How? Just look in the almanac you prefer, for charts that show the cost of health care by nations and how long people live in those countries.

Test across time: In most countries that have socialized medical care, the cost is much less than the cost in the U.S., without any apparent health crisis. In countries that have what we call socialized health care, such as France, Germany, Britain, Italy, Australia, and Sweden, the costs are less than in the U.S., yet life expectancy is not reduced. Life expectancy in the U.S. is 77.9 years. In France it is 78.6 years, in Germany 78.6 years, in Britain 78.3 years, in Italy 80 years, in Austria 80.2 years, and in Sweden 80.6 years.[1]

Unless you want to argue that long life isn't a good measure of the quality of health care, you might want to reevaluate your position on government supported health care.

Although at this moment the U.S. economy is doing reasonably well, sooner or later we will have more problems. Inflation (rapidly rising prices

across a wide economic sector) and other issues will cause people to call for
the government to control prices and wages in order to control inflation. How
can we tell if this is a good idea? Try comparative analysis:

Create a hypothesis.

A. Hypothesis: Government wage and price controls will work well to control wages and prices.
B. Test by looking back across time and see what has happened when wage
   and price controls are enacted.

Wage and price controls have been used since the Roman times, two thousand years ago. This may not have been a good thing for the Romans, but it
is great for students wishing to do a comparative analysis. We can quickly
learn that the result of such policies has been almost universal failure. The
best result seen in history is a temporary stop to the rapid rise in prices, but
this is usually followed by future rises and distortions in the economy. The
only exception seems to be in time of war, during which the people are willing to help the government enforce the rules. Knowing what does happen
when you impose wage and price controls might help you to decide if, as a
citizen, you want the government to impose such laws.

Remember: In the social sciences, we have trouble giving definitive
answers—we can only accumulate evidence that supports our hypothesis or
reduces support for our hypothesis.

Here is another example of where comparative analysis might help:

Fran Wood, in the Newark, N.J., Star-Ledger, wrote an article entitled
"Leave No Group Behind." Wood reported the view of Caroline Elders, professor of Education at Rutgers University's Graduate School of Education
that some groups are falling behind because we haven't sufficiently addressed
the "twin barriers of language and culture." Prof. Elders said, "If you come to
this country not speaking the language, and you go into a [school] that doesn't
take that into account, you're not going to succeed." Let us apply some quick
acting comparative analysis.

According to all the statistics I have ever seen, most Asians came to
America not speaking English as their first language or speaking it at all,
yet they rank higher than native speakers generally in GPA, SAT scores,
level of education, achieved, and about any other measure of academic
achievement you might name. If you are a good citizen, feel free to change
your mind.

Let's apply some more comparative analysis to the professor's proposi-
tion. Wood observes that most Jews came to this country from non-English-
speaking countries. Judging by the number of business successes, profes-

sors, and intellectuals who are Jewish, I am inclined to think that it is good for immigrants to speak English when they come, but it is not the most important element for success.[2] According to some researchers who follow the results of standardized test scores, there isn't much of a relationship between school expenditure and school performance.[3]

If this is true, then perhaps the heaviest weight of responsibility for student success should be placed on the student. This goes against the politically correct view that we, society and government are responsible for a student's performance in school. Since I have had very few problems made worse by more money, I don't like it when people say that money doesn't matter. Usually it does help. It seems obvious that in education, other factors, such as hours spent studying, matter more.

Mistakes in analysis occur when the one doing the analyzing brings dogmatic agenda to the process. People we might label "liberal" have a view that emphasizes the role and efficacy of government. When this framework is applied to education, it always spins out the same result: The problem is outside of the individual's power to change and needs to be fixed by the government.

Freddy Ferrer ran for Mayor in New York City, emphasizing education. He repeatedly said that many students hadn't made progress on the tests used to measure such progress. He never once mentioned students' responsibility, and not that many people remembered him at the polls. Liberals think that conservatives are nut balls who are only interested in repressing sexual behavior, but many voters, whatever their political leanings, know that personal responsibility belongs in all of life, including intimate relationships.[4]

In New Jersey, the State Supreme Court is a confident court and often leads in decisions that are heralded by the most progressive elements in our society. For over thirty years, the court has taken upon itself the task of telling the people of New Jersey how they must finance the state schools and allocate money to them. The court decrees that the state must give the poorest districts enough money to equalize opportunity and achievement. This means that some middle class parents spend more money to educate other people's children than they spend to educate their own children. Children in the disadvantaged areas automatically go to preschool, although there is zero evidence that this improves ultimate academic performance. Parents in other districts pay for these preschoolers, even if they can't afford to send their own children to preschool.[5]

Of the 603 districts in New Jersey, 583 spend less per pupil than does the Newark system, yet the Newark schools don't have high scores on any known form of test. Schools that spend thousands less, such as Mountain Lakes and Holmdel, have much higher scores. Nor has education appreciably changed since the court stepped in to bring equality to school spending. Students in Newark and elsewhere are doing about as well as they were doing before the court starting running the system.[6]

Let us look at some of the ideas that may be sitting around in our heads drinking lemonade and having a good old time.

Newspapers and other media give the perception that the more violent and interesting crimes are being committed in New York City and Detroit. One might reasonably conclude that cities have more crime than other places and that something about cities stimulates criminal behavior, perhaps because cities are so crowded. The close proximity of the rich and poor, maybe gives opportunity for crime. Perhaps the dog-eat-dog attitude that prevails in the city is a factor, or maybe just the sheer wear and tear on nerves rubbed raw by bumping up against so many others.

But actually, comparative analysis calls such theses into question. Large cities such as New York City have lower crime rates per capita than other less populous places. Also, one hears more about New York City crime because the city is a center of media, and reporters tend to cover what is local more than what is far away. Also, since more people in the cities are news consumers, it pays for the media to cover what interests them.

Start comparative analysis of the ideas with the test of space. We want to look for places that have high population density and low rates of crime. How about the Netherlands? People in the lowlands have so little land that they must reclaim land from the sea using dikes and such. The U.S. Department of State, however, considers violent crimes to be of little concern in the Netherlands. As with much of Europe, purse snatchings and pickpockets are a serious problem in crowded tourist areas.[7]

What about Japan? It is about the size of the state of California. They have a very low rate of crime.

Look at what you have accomplished. You have enough evidence to make reasonable and open-minded people think twice about the theory that overcrowding leads to more crime. Or you can just go back to the theory you love so well, and no one will bother you. You have done your duty and richly deserve the love you will make tonight if you engage in some comparative analysis.

Many conservatives say that a high rate of government spending is not good for the economy. Certainly, when the government controls the entire economy, the economy drops over a cliff. We may suspect that too large a commitment to the welfare state entails severe economic costs. Some European governments have come to the conclusion that taxes and government services must be cut or these nations will fall further behind America in productivity and living conditions. But perhaps some conservatives are coming to "worship" lower taxes. Some conservatives talk as if the market is all knowing and always correct in making decisions on who gets what. This may be true if the only goal is efficiency, but that leaves morality out of the considerations. Remember that the Eskimos used to place their elderly loved ones on a piece of ice and watch them float out to sea when it was time to go. If you really believe only efficiency counts, go now and tell your grandmother about her ice chunk hospice.

The conservative view is that high government spending inevitably hurts the economy. The hypothesis: The more the government spending, the less healthy and efficient the economy.

We will test our hypothesis by looking at space-time events. Studies show what part of the national wealth is paid to the central government. By looking at such a chart, we can easily see that the only two industrial democracies that spend much less than the European countries are Japan and the United States. The United States is currently doing well economically. Japan has its occasional problems, but the country is always in the top tier of economies. Credit must be given for rebuilding after World War II. So it seems that you can spend just a little money through the government and be prosperous. So far, folks, it seems as if you can have low taxes and a prosperous economy.

Unfortunately, for people who have a death grip on the idea that lower taxation is always better, there is a problem: Two dozen countries in Europe are also prosperous. The countries of Western Europe are more or less in the same category of wealthy nations as the United States. Some are not as prosperous as the United States, but they still are among the world's healthiest economies. Some European countries that aren't healthy yet seem on a track to arrive in the top tier after another generation. Canada has a lot more government benefits but seems to be rather well off.

While some conservatives wait for the end of the world to arrive in Sweden and other high tax countries, so far this has not happened. European countries continue to be democratic and prosperous. Lately it is becoming clear that they must cut back on their benefits to be globally competitive, but even after cutbacks they will still have more generous benefits than the U. S. We have already given the example of Germany in the decades after World War II. Germans made an economic recovery to become the strongest economy in Europe. Germany had the highest percentage of spending by a central government of all the governments in Europe. This would seem to be good evidence that an involved government can still have a strong economy.

A reasonable conclusion is that the exact role of the government in the economy isn't entirely clear. The comparative analysis of national economies does show that the government that totally controls the economy is headed for disaster. The trick is to find the right level of government activity. Some on the right may say that lower involvement is always better but there isn't much evidence to back it up. Some on the left might always say that the more government the better.

Since President Ronald Reagan, fewer and fewer folks say that in America unless they have tenure. How do we know what amount of government spending is right? We don't, but a fair-minded person would have to say that America is on a faster track to prosperity than is most of Europe, so less government seems better for the moment. As we watch countries exercise too much or too little government control, we may be able to provide more accurate predictors. As long as we don't have government by dogmatic-fools, we should be okay.

Medical care is another topic too often illuminated by more heat than light. Social liberals say that 46 million people in the U.S. are without medical care. This isn't true. Actually, 45.8 million people are without medical insurance, according to the U.S. Census Bureau.[8] Lately, some have become concerned that the media are now wise to this semantic nuance and are repeating it less often. Social conservatives say that socialized medicine, however it is defined, means that everyone in the country has guaranteed medical insurance. Many people think that socialized medical care will result in ever-increasing costs and ever-decreasing quality of care.

As I promised, comparative analysis is powerful stuff that can be used to annoy those on either the right or the left. In the case of national health care, the trick is to find whether countries with socialized medical care spend more or less than the United States does, and whether people in countries that have socialized medical care are as healthy.

I take my *World Almanac* in the left hand and use my right hand to thumb the index. I suspect that "Health and Medicine" will be the place to look. Under this category I see "Expenditures" on page 83, 98, and 122. I write these down and I go to those pages. Page 83 only has the U.S. expenditures. So I turn to page 98. On page 98 I see a chart with the heading "Spending on Health in the 50 Most Populous Countries." We can see that the U.S. spends much more on health care than nearly all other nations.

Measuring the health of U.S. citizens in general requires looking at a lot of factors. The National Center for Health Statistics has gathered all of these in a single resource, *Health: United States.*[9]

From time to time the economy will suffer from inflationary pressures, which means a rapid, across-the-board increase in prices. When this happens, people often ask the government to take action (beyond influencing the economy through the Federal Reserve System). The most frequent suggestion is to enact wage and price controls, which means that the government dictates wages paid to workers and the prices of items for sale in the marketplace.

This is not the case today, of course, but it will happen in time. You could be ready to deal with this issue by applying the comparative method to analyze whether to use wage and price controls in the economy. You will have a measure of objectivity to your analysis that will be welcome by me and everyone who is not an ideological fool. First, we frame the hypothesis: Government wage and price controls are effective in stopping inflation.

Second, we test our model of our world view (the hypothesis) by looking back in time and in different places in the world. Luckily for us, Inflation through the Ages: Economic, Social, Psychological and Historical Aspects has gone back over a two-thousand-year period to find that wage and price controls almost never work, regardless of the good intentions of the government.[10] After the government imposes price controls there may be a temporary stop to rising prices but this will be followed by rapid rises when controls are removed. Perhaps a nation's economy is too complex and ambiguous to be controlled by any particular set of rules.

For example: A government wants to control the price of a sheet of plywood. It sets the price. Then it sets a higher price for a "moderately finished" piece of plywood. I, the manufacturer, want a higher price for the plywood, so I drill three holes in the end of a piece of plywood and call it a moderately finished piece of plywood and charge a higher price. Whether anyone actually uses the three holes is of no importance. The government has given a way to raise the prices. The buyer probably won't care, as long as he can get a usable piece of plywood.

Since a rigid price on a product usually results in a shortage, I will soon be able to sell all my pieces of plywood including the ones with three holes at a higher price than the government will wish. People usually can scoot around government rules faster than any government can make them. There are those who believe that if the government gets rough enough or thorough enough, it can control anything it wishes to control. Perhaps, but try to find an example. There is evidence that the government can have a fair amount of success if the people overwhelmingly agree with the importance of price control. The best example is during a popular war such as World War II. But war is a heavy price to pay to stabilize prices.

Comparative analysis is a powerful tool. It quickly provides clear evidence that someone should at least reconsider their point of view. Perhaps it should come with a warning label saying "Be careful: The view you should reconsider might be your own." Urging others to reconsider their views can ruin a friendship forever, particularly if you like to be with those who hold their political views with fervor. Once taught to students, it can be brought around to devastate the ideology of the professor. Students are usually too afraid to speak up and challenge the professor but, if this method is taught by the professor, it may just be the bit of confidence they need to become thinking rebels.

Chapter Three

Opposing Views

You may or may not feel passionate about a particular issue, but whatever the issue, someone somewhere probably does feel passion when talking about it. Someone will bring all their intelligence and energy to bear in the necessary research to support their point of view. This is good news.

In almost every area of life, there are opposing points of view. Regarding public policy, the sides can usually be reduced to some form of liberalism or conservatism.

In the United States, the tendency of liberals, according to the *Stanford Encyclopedia of Philosophy* (2007) is to argue that equality must be protected. Each person is to have an equal rights and opportunities. A problem arises if the government ends up trying to level the playing field by reaching into every corner where inequality lurks.

In practice, the demands of equalizing society require a large, intrusive government. For the government, for example, to know which person to provide with special opportunities, it must become all knowing and all intrusive. How will it be able to compare the pain suffered by someone of a particular color with the pain suffered by someone whose father was an alcoholic? How will it compare a person who grew up in poverty with someone whose mother was in a concentration camp? How will it compare someone whose mother was killed by the communists with someone who has a clubfoot? How will it compare someone of a race that suffered in the United States but was born in Haiti, with someone whose father left when he was ten?

For the government to start favoring one person over another based on pain suffered, it would seem that the government must acquire God-like powers, or rely on an ideology that subjectively pronounces people worthy of support or not, based on such general characteristics as race or gender. Such unjustified distinctions raise questions that cannot be answered, so the government must silence those who object, perhaps by calling them a racist or sexist.

Or perhaps the government could just favor the one group, black Americans, whose suffering in this country is widely acknowledged to be a special case. This might be done because most Americans want to assist black Americans get to where they would have been if they hadn't suffered for centuries. In practice this is difficult, since everyone who has acquired special privileges does not want to give them up.

Other people are conservative. Their attitude distrusts government attempts to change the status quo in order to bring equality. In general, the political or social conservative is fearful of unintended consequences and of undermining traditional institutions that seem to work. While liberals stress equality, conservatives stress liberty, the freedom to act without interference and to either succeed or fail. Both viewpoints have eloquent defenders and sources that disseminate their own platform and vision. Liberals tend to like *The New York Times.* Conservatives prefer the *Wall Street Journal.* Those who wish to be well informed read both.

As Yogi Berra said, "You can learn a lot just by reading." When your real life gets going after college, you may think that you don't have time to look things up in an almanac, let alone take five minutes to look things up in the *Statistical Abstract* or anything more sophisticated. If so, there is a lot to gain simply by reading several national publications and surfing the Web for different views.

Reading another point of view may convince us that, yes, we were right all along. But reading another point of view may force us to change some or all of our views. Or, heaven forbid, force us to come up with better arguments to support our own view. At the very least, we won't be surprised by the views of those who take disparate views of things.

I have been told that if you want to write a best-selling book that deals with politics you should avoid all nuances and take a confident stand. It doesn't matter what stand you take?just be confident about it. I would like to do that, but the fact is, I find that there are a lot of people who are brighter and more imaginative than I am. Thus I am often startled to find that "Wow, I hadn't though of that." Apparently, however, people don't like to think that someone else might have an insight they like, so they must force themselves to listen to opposing views. The best way to do this, I think, is to read articles by people who are almost guaranteed to have different points of view. For example, a person whose views are to the left can read the editorial page of the *Wall Street Journal.*

Here's an example: The federal government lowered estate taxes. There are valid arguments for and against doing this. One of the more powerful for eliminating taxes is the story that people have been forced to give up farms that had been in the family for generations so that they might pay high estate taxes. The story goes that, after the death of a farm owner, the farm is sold because the children cannot afford to pay the taxes. Because of rising land prices, the farm is worth millions, but farms don't earn a great deal of money, so the children who wanted to continue farming can't because the taxes cost more than they can earn.

However, according to *The New York Times,* this story is a myth. One well known tax law expert and professor at Iowa State University said he could not find a single case in which a farm was lost because of estate taxes."[1]

Many stories similar to the "We will lose the farm" myth make the rounds. This is one reason many pictures in our heads are so often wrong. We keep them there because it doesn't cost anything. As a friend said to me, incorrect assumptions don't cost much and they don't eat much. The government doesn't send around a fact checker to see how accurate the pictures in our head are. It might cost time and effort to find out if that picture is accurate. Meanwhile, you're busy. A paper is due in three days, you are running out of money, and your girlfriend doesn't close her eyes when you kiss her lips anymore. There is much to do and the pictures in your head are not bothering anyone. Why bother? Unless being a rational citizen becomes a priority, there isn't any good reason.

The March 23, 1995, *New York Times* provided a chart on the dawn of a new era when welfare was being reformed. Looking at all the facts, you may be surprised to learn that there are more whites than blacks on welfare. Perhaps you think that the cost is higher or lower than the given state and federal cost of $25 billion. Perhaps you have an image in your mind of large numbers of children trailing a mother. But the average welfare family size, including the mother, is 2.9. You learn that the main reason for going on welfare is divorce or out-of-wedlock childbirth, which is what mothers have been telling their dating daughters for generations.

Here are examples of stories that might be good to read if you take an opposing view of the conventional wisdom.

The Accountability Project was begun by AIDS patient Michael Petrelis, because he became angry when he found out how much AIDS organizations pay their executives. In the article you would find that nonprofits are a trillion dollar industry.[2] In 1998, Petrelis found twenty-one executives at ten of the top AIDS charities who had pay packages exceeding $100,000. Jerome Radwin, a director of the American Foundation for AIDS Research in New York made $181,000, but he wasn't the highest paid AIDS executive. That honor belonged to Walden House executive director Alfonso Acampora.[3] It is up to you to decide whether this salary is too high or low. I think you will agree that this number is food for thought.

Martin Gross was angry about what he considers foolish spending by the government. He wrote *The Government Racket: Washington Waste from A to Z* (2000), which covered such expenditures as a $19 million to study cow flatulence (I only wish I had the imagination to make this up) and $57,000 to provide embossed playing cards for Air Force One, the U.S. president's personal plane. My personal favorite is $500,000 to build a replica of the Great Pyramid of Giza in Indiana.[4]

Look at the two letters in the February 26, 2003, issue of *The New York Times* regarding the February 25 article "U.S. Crackdown Sets off Unusual Rush to Canada." Two people have written about the same situation from totally different views about who is responsible. One says that the U.S. government should look more closely at illegal immigrants who come from countries associated with terrorists, and be wary of allowing them to enter the U.S. The other says the U.S. government is at fault and is unnecessarily harassing harmless people.

During the war in Afghanistan and Iraq, a spate of stories covered women in the military. Some were stimulated by the apparent heroic acts of Jessica Lynch. For another point of view, look at "Men, Women, and the War" in the March 24, 1999, issue of the *Wall Street Journal*.[5] An open-minded person needs to read both articles, not just the one that backs their point of view.

When emotions run high about a particular issue, take more time to read opposing points of view. This is when partisans feel obligated to support their side, regardless of the facts. If you only read one source, or one side, you will be in danger of just absorbing ideology. Ideology depends on how you hold the information. If you allow yourself to openly examine facts or ideas counter to your views then I would call your data information, but if your data or ideas must conform to your worldview or be discarded, then I would call your particular point dogma. If there is enough to constitute a worldview, I would call it ideology.

Emotions have been running high for decades regarding the issue of affirmative action. Institutions practicing affirmative action have policies that are consciously discriminatory in favor of some group that has been identified as needing special consideration. Usually the group that benefits from affirmative action is thought to have suffered from past bigotry. Some see affirmative action as important in promoting the welfare of a group that has been abused; others see this as a subtle form of bigotry that looks at individuals only as part of a group.

In 1991, the supporters of affirmative action were delighted when two pro-fessors at the University of California, Davis, found that affirmative action medical school students were able to succeed. Some may have noted that the story also said that students "receiving admissions preferences—not all of which were members of minorities—performed less well in the basic sciences courses of the first two years." However, *The Times* and others were gener-ally well-pleased with the results which were trumpeted as evidence that af-firmative action worked while hurting no one.[6]

A doctor from another university, who was also a trustee of the American Medical Association, went so far as to say that "this is a highly significant study, what I would call a landmark study." The article had a smaller headline saying "Similar Academic Reports, Similar Careers." *The New York Times* is a ferocious supporter of affirmative action, but it is also thought of by most people as the newspaper of record. Therefore, many people probably thought there was no need to critique the essential meaning of the story.[7]

Still, it might be worth a look to see what opponents had to say. Luckily, there is usually an easy way to do this comparison of different views. In this great country, the two best and most influential newspapers are *The New York Times* and the *Wall Street Journal,* which often take opposite positions on the news. For most people, reading both newspapers on a regular basis is sufficient to be able to offer reasoned and valid opinions on just about any issue of pub-lic policy. The person who reads both papers will be better informed and more likely to think with clarity. Certainly the citizen who has arrived at a conclu-sion after looking at both sides will fare better than one who has not. Although this is an era that demands little of citizens, I think that reasoning after hear-ing from both sides can be an important mark of being a good citizen.

Here is an example of this viewpoint comparison. You don't have to agree with the following story. I just want to provide an example of going against the grain. At this time, emotions are running high regarding what to do about terrorism. Most want protection but do not wish to trample on anyone's civil liberties. Michelle Malkin wrote *In Defense of Internment: The World War II Roundup and What It Means for the War on Terror* to explore President Franklin D. Roosevelt's order, at the start of World War II, to move ethnic Japanese from the coasts of the United States.[8] After the attacks of 2001, the memory of Japanese internment caused a stir among advocates for a vigorous war against Islamist terrorism. Most everyone seems to know that there is only one side to this story: Out of the vilest racism, we acted in a racist and unjust way to imprison innocent Japanese people.

Few would argue that the U.S. in 1941 was a good deal more racist than it is today. But what if recruits of Imperial Japan had set up a spy network in

America, staffed with people who could provide information on West Coast military bases? Among the displaced Japanese, 1648 had actually been soldiers in the Imperial Army. More than five thousand Japanese-Americans renounced their U.S. citizenship, and 2031 returned to Japan before the end of the war. More than fourteen thousand German and Italian aliens also were interned. These facts may not justify internment camps, but they put the action in context. Given the current political climate in the U.S., anyone who denies that racism was the supreme factor in setting up the internment camps is going to need a good deal of internal fortitutde.[9]

Most historians discount the importance of Japanese propaganda aimed at rallying support among Japanese in America and recruit them as spies. No one I know of has said that any of the other information is false. How many know that fourteen thousand Germans and Italians also were interned? That was far fewer than the Japanese interned but still a sizable number. Was it all just a question of racism? Even in the most emotionally divisive situations, another side may warrant consideration. There is a free country inside your head.

Lately, many people have turned their righteous wrath against SUVs. I am somewhat sympathetic to their cause. We are trying to be more independent of Middle East oil supplies, yet people are driving inefficient trucks of military design heritage. On my long commute, I dislike SUVs because it is hard to see past them to upcoming turns, exits, and toll plazas. Of course, I could just be jealous because I don't have enough money to afford buy and drive one.

Here is a letter from someone in Blairstown, New Jersey, who points out an embarrassing notion. He asks: "Why be so angry about SUVs? . . . How about taxing home heating oil for all those hot shots with five thousand-square-foot castles that overlook the huddle masses driving their gas guzzlers." Good point. How large are the homes of the liberal stars? Don't some own more than one house? Is their house cold in the winter? It does seem that we sometimes pick our targets to suit our need to be self-righteous while avoiding blame ourselves.

In the search for opposing points of view, you will notice a pattern and become adept at spotting counterpoints to your argument. You will learn, for example, that capital punishment is a hot button issue that never fails to get *The New York Times* excited. After the Supreme Court excluded juvenile offenders from those eligible for the death penalty, *The Times* had an article in its March 2, 2005, issue, "Court Takes Another Step in Reshaping Capital Punishment." The article cheerfully anticipated the end of the death penalty.

The *Wall Street Journal,* which doesn't talk much about the death penalty but dislikes judicial activism, had an editorial on its WSJ.com Web site, "The Blue State Court" with the headlines "The Justices Continue Their Social Activism." The *Journal* article argues that "a narrow majority of Justices" has been imposing its own blue-state cultural mores on the rest of the country." If you favor those mores, you may not care. This comment may make you think that perhaps the next time you vote, you will vote to put more of the power to make policy decisions in the democratically elected branch of government. That is up to you. By reading the two most influential newspapers, you will probably be better educated in current events.

Unfortunately, it is most important to check the other side's view precisely when the emotional heat is at its height. Fortunately, as is said on the most interesting of the late night television offers, all this can be done in the privacy of your own home.

The New York Times does seem to have a point in its observation that the U.S. Supreme Court seems to be moving rapidly toward eliminating capital punishment. Recent restrictions have been added in rulings that have eliminated capital punishment for the mentally impaired and for people who commit crimes when they are not yet sixteen. Numerous articles and studies argue that we should stop all capital punishment because there is a good chance that we are making mistakes and executing innocent people.

The counterpoint is taken by Professor of Law Paul Cassell. He claims that stories of executing the innocent are driven by an ideological agenda.[10] At the time of this article, former presidential candidate Al Gore had cited a particular study that said the capital punishment system is collapsing under its own weight. His proof was a 68 percent "error rate" in convictions where the death penalty was imposed. According to Cassell, the 68 percent statistic has nothing to do with executing the right or wrong person. The author of the study reviewed executions over twenty-three years of capital sentences and did not find a single case in which a person was proven innocent after being executed.

So where does this 68 percent doodle come from? "It turns out to include any reversal of a capital sentence at any stage by appellate courts, even if those courts uphold the capital sentence." Thus if, for example, an appellate court asks for additional findings and, after rereading the material, affirms the sentence, the report will count this as an error, to be counted with the 68 percent error rate.[11]

Perhaps no area is more emotionally volatile in public policy debate than HIV-AIDS. Support for money going to research and patient care is a litmus test for one's humanity. Questioning any position taken by HIV-AIDS advocates is taken as certain evidence that one is evil. Nonetheless, some people have spoken up, noting that the attitude toward this disease is different than that exhibited toward any other disease.

The traditional standard of dealing with similar diseases is that every case must be located, reported and its source ascertained. Contacts must be found and informed about the possibility of infection. Gabriel Rotello deals with what has become known as "AIDS exceptionalism."[12] Those with the HIV virus have been subjected to discrimination. Still, the practical benefits of stopping the spread of HIV-AIDS should override some other sensibilities.

For example, in New Jersey, prospective mothers cannot be tested without permission. HIV-AIDS victims are allowed to continue infecting others. Charles Harris, who is seeking to end the special status given to HIV victims, states, "Plagues cannot be contained unless their source is documented."[13]

The feature film *Munich,* directed by Steven Spielberg, stirred controversy for its depiction of terrorist and counterterrorist tactics. This is either a brilliant movie that provides a fair and balanced view of the best approach to ending violence, or it is a biased view that is historically incorrect, and it advocates views that have not been successful in stopping violence by fanatics. For a view that "militant attempts to destroy terrorism lead not to peace but to cycles of violence . . . and that opposing sides [in the battle over terrorism] begin to resemble each other," you can check in with *The New York Times* article, "A Massacre in Munich, and What Came After" by Janet Maslin.[14] Or go to "Seeing terrorism as Drama With Sequels and Prequels."[15] Such articles are conveniently placed in various editions of *The New York Times.*

Spielberg presents the message in his film that terrorism is not destroyed by force. Edward Rothstein, who occasionally writes politically incorrect essays in *The Times,* lists numerous occasions in which terrorism indeed was destroyed by force.[16]

When oil prices and gas prices climb rapidly, every newscast has at least one story on the matter. This story happens every summer, because prices rise every summer. People sitting in their cars in a gas station often were interviewed. They agreed that, yes, prices were high, and they were unhappy about it. Immediately, politicians said that the prices were an outrage, and we needed to look into it and see if the oil companies were making windfall profits.

Since I should follow my own rules and looked at history, I knew that this had happened before. When it did, either the government got involved, resulting in shortages and lines at the gas stations or the politicians blustered and after a short time the price subsided. But the *Wall Street Journal* had an editorial on November 2, 2005, in which they asked if stopping people from getting windfall profits meant that we would take some of the money many people had recently made from selling their houses for hundreds of thousands of dollars they could not have gotten until the very recent price rise. They also mentioned other areas of great profits, such as making a blockbuster movie. This discussion brought home the thought that "windfall profits" are profits that other people make. Overcharging on something that is a necessity also is considered especially evil. But is buying gas really a necessity? Is it necessary to heat a large home where rooms are unused? Reading both sides helps sort this out.

Love your enemies for they shall make your life easier. Here is a good example: You are often fuming that the chief executives of corporations are always getting away with murder. You are a good person who is too busy with your own life to spend a lot of time finding data that backs up your point of view, but you know you are right. If you have been wise enough to buy this book and also to subscribe to *The New York Times* and the *Wall Street Journal,* you will soon find data for your arguments in both of these papers and even be able to quote from those with whom you disagree.

Saying that you read in *The New York Times* that we should end corporate subsidies or that corporate chiefs are doing bad things impresses no one. Why would *The Times* say anything else? It would be more impressive if you could quote from the *Wall Street Journal* that the government should assign a commission to "identify and eliminate the estimated $100 billion a year in corporate welfare subsidies."[17]

Sometimes a particular view is just not mentioned because it differs from the prevailing worldview of the "enlightened ones." One such view is that we are doomed by having too many people alive on the planet, and many millions will starve unless we feed the poor. At the moment we are having the latest version the millennium project, which seeks to raise awareness of the plight of the poor and have more give more. This is a fine idea.

But what if there were a better way? There is. Norman Borlaug won the 1970 Nobel Peace Prize for being the father of the green revolution. This revolution made it possible for food hungry nations like India and Pakistan to feed their people by planting grains that were genetically engineered to be hardier and produced several times more than the previously available varieties. Later, other researchers built on Borlaug's ideas, producing super varieties of rice.[18]

Why don't we hear more of this giant who saved so many lives? Is it because he has shown the world that, with a semi-sane government, no one needs to go to bed hungry? I suspect it is for the same reason that few of us have ever seen or heard about Rosalyn Yalow, the 1977 winner of a Nobel Peace Prize for her achievements regarding nuclear medicine. Dr. Yalow has an unfortunate tendency to promote nuclear energy as a potential savior rather than an endless menace.[19] If that isn't bad enough, she also advises women scientists to stop complaining and just get on with the research.

When certain facts have been ignored, reading points of view for the different positions can instantly eliminate arguments. You may not enjoy this process but it is better to have this happen in the privacy of your own home than in public.

In the U.S. illegal alien debate, the plan to grant "amnesty" to undocumented workers stirred a storm of protest. Those who argued for an amnesty plan taunted their opponents with the impracticality of deporting 10 million people. Instead of having the audience picture a long and sad line of 10 million people, you can, if you have read the opponents of amnesty, say: "No one is suggesting mass deportation for 10 million people. Reliable and consistent enforcement of existing laws should lead to the steadily dwindling of the illegal immigrant population over several years. All we have to do is make illegal immigration unprofitable for the undocumented workers and their employers."

Chapter Four

Personal Experience

Experience should count for something. This is an opportunity to use your subjective experience. Since it has caused you a lot of pain to create a good deal of your experience, it should be good news that it can help you as well. The goal is not a scientific experiment; it is a chance to argue with a policy decision that depends on such matters as human nature.

This method isn't decisive, but it can cause you to question the position you hold. Sometimes you are one of the people that policy makers are talking about. Sometimes you are not. The idea is to wrestle with the material.

Example: There is a plan to let your generation invest all or part of U.S. citizens' Social Security savings in the stock market. Let us say that we want to know if this policy has a good chance of becoming a law. How do you feel about trading some certainty for a chance of greater gain? Most people would like the opportunity to double the amount of money they will receive from Social Security. However, in our experience, the stock market goes down as well as up. Do you want to risk your Social Security money? By talking about it, you can get a sense of what other people are thinking.

What is the best way to slow down population growth? Using yourself as the case study, ask,

- How many children did my grandparents have?
- How many children do I want to have?
- What are the differences that change this desire between my grandparents and myself? Is it rising income and education? Do you think these would have the same effect on others?

Personal experience can make significant differences in how people relate to the world around them. A $5 bill looks a lot different to someone who has lived in poverty all of her life and one who has a billionaire grandfather. In a negative way, this hit home when I learned that a program I thought was a good idea turned out to be a disappointment.

Can young people be scared into giving up criminal behavior? I thought so after seeing *Scared Straight,* a 1978 documentary filmed at East Jersey State Prison in Rahway, New Jersey. A group of men serving life sentences confront a group of repeat-offender teens, ages thirteen to nineteen. The boys have been given a choice by the courts: They can avoid doing jail time if they spend a day with the lifers in prison." The men tell what prison life is like in the most graphic detail, and by the end of the film the boys have decided they would just as soon walk the straight and narrow. The film won an Academy Award for documentaries, and it was followed up with studies done ten years and twenty years later. Evidently the tactic worked well on the original group of boys.

The idea caught on quickly, and teen offenders were soon getting the treatment at East Jersey and other prisons across the land. Scared Straight has received publicity and support.

Based on the experiences of the first juveniles, who went through the program in the 1970s, the approach was effective. Based on my experience, I assumed that it would be very effective. My own reaction in seeing videos of these sessions was that they sure scared me straighter than I was before. The very thought of being in a confined space with a lonely man named Bubba who is wider than a double wide refrigerator, sure made me sit up and take notice. The stories of violence, of being unable to defend yourself no matter how big and strong you are, and the unceasing stories of humiliation and depression should be enough to make everyone stay straight.

However, personal experience is affected by various things. Some researchers have questioned whether a social shift has even occurred in the subculture of juvenile offenders. What could still frighten in the 1970s actually has the opposite effect on violent teens in the new millennium. Some believe the program actually has begun to encourage further criminality in those who go through it instead of less.

How could this be? I can only look at how my own experience guides my perceptions. It is dangerous if I expect everyone else's experiences, worldview, and values to bring them to the same reality I see. For example: Why would young men strap explosive onto their bodies and detonate themselves, taking out as many men, women, and children as possible? That experience grid is not one with which I can identify.

Regarding the Scared Straight Program's message, it couldn't have found a more receptive set of experiences than mine. I grew up in a nice suburb. Our back yard adjoined that of the chief of police. He was a nice man who always threw the baseball back when it went into his yard. He gave out the neatest candy to trick-or-treaters at Halloween. Coming out of such a culture, if I am in a crowd and a policeman yells, I always stop, even if I haven't done anything bad for three months. But I am not a part of the audience who needs to be shaken up by Bubba. Even if my initial view might have been wrong it is still worthwhile using your own experience to think about public policies. There are times when your own experiences will also be the wrong guide, but it is usually worthwhile to see if your experiences can help you to understand a current situation.

So, experience does count for something. It is certainly a factor that we should take with us into analyzing the world's problems. If we are talking to or about people who come from generally the same background as ourselves, experience can be quite helpful. But as the Scared Straight promoters discovered, sometimes experiences are too different to help. Experiences sometimes can actually lead us away from reality.

The other major contribution of our experiences is the development of our personal views. For many people, an ongoing source of their views is a worldview. This is a broad view that contains many generalizations about the world. A good example would be a person who is religious. Religion leads them to view history as something that has meaning and purpose. They would have a specific view of salvation. There would be a view of human nature. For example, can people change? How does change come about? What is the appropriate role of government in creating and changing character? Will people always be a combination of good and evil? How important is this life? This worldview could also include views about current topics such as abortion or feeding the hungry.

For many people, it is an ideological position that helps determine their views on current topics. For example, a person who is a Marxist would emphasize the role of economics in determining what matters and what should be done about specific problems. Someone who is a Freudian would emphasize the role of the unconscious and sex in understanding the world, as well as determining their stand on current issues.

A person could be someone who is greatly influenced by views currently popular in academic settings, such as post-modernism. This view has great faith in the ability of humans to construct a better society where secondary characteristics of humans beings, such as their race, class and gender do not influence how we relate to one another. They might also believe that enlightened elite can bring about a better world.

Many worldviews have been used throughout history. The methods in this book aim at having people take an objective view of current public policies regardless of their worldview.

Whatever position you hold is closely tied to your views on public policy. You can gain a greater understanding of that position if you examine how your personal world view has impacted that position in respect to a given issue.

Chapter Five

The Numbers

Often with a few simple arithmetic calculations you can get a better understanding of government decisions. The U.S. federal government deals with very large numbers. You get a better sense of the amount of spending by working the numbers yourself.

The U.S. Budget is in the *World Almanac*. Find answers to the questions . . .

- How much does the federal government spend an hour?
- How much does the federal government spend a minute?
- How much does the federal government spend a second?

Do the math and look at the answers. Do they surprise you? Do they alter your thinking?

At this writing, the U.S. national government budget is around $2.285 trillion. The number is so large it is meaningless for most citizens. But divide by 365, and you learn that at this level the government spends $6.26 billion a day. To put it in perspective, a billion seconds ago we were celebrating the bicentennial year and a billion minutes ago Trajan was the emperor of Rome. It's a damn big number!

I also have no idea what billions of dollars looks like, but we can at least dare to think about this number. How is it possible to spend $6.26 billion a day and have so many problems? I am at a loss to provide a good answer, because it seems a few days of that kind of spending should make things better. Whether or not the money helps, a little arithmetic has helped me understand government a little better.

An important public policy issue is social security. Older people often want to receive more money from their Social Security checks, and it often seems cruel not to give them more money. As the holiday season approaches, a politician might ask, "Why not give the elderly one more dollar for Christmas?"

How much would this cost? According to the *World Almanac,* in April 2007, the Social Security Administration counted 46,964,000 recipients. Therefore,

$1 = \$46,964,000$
$2 = \$93,928,000$
$3 = \$140,892,000$

Once again, a little wrestling with the numbers gives some understanding.

A number of insurance companies, hospitals, and a liberal consumer group brought forth a proposal for a program to provide health insurance for about half the U.S. citizens who lack health insurance. In 2005, it was 45.8 million, according to Census Bureau statistics. Assuming that it costs about $1 billion a year to provide health insurance coverage for 1 million low-income people, let's work some numbers.

The level of coverage in this particular plan would cost $45.8 billion.[1] You now have a number. You might compare this to other expenditures in the budget, which you will also find in the *Almanac.* You might be surprised at how low (for a country) this number is. You might be alarmed at how high it is. At least you are thinking in a factual manner that is within anyone's grasp. As simple as this is to do, it is rarely done.

There are other questions you might ask, such as, "How many people are left without coverage? How much money should each person be earning before we say that they should provide their own coverage?"

The above proposal would help families who earn up to twice the amount of income specified as the poverty level. For a family of three, the poverty threshold is $16,090 (2005 figures).[2] Work the numbers. This family would be helped if it earned up to $28,300. Is this too little or to much to help others who are without insurance? How high will you go and how much will it increase your taxes? These are important questions but now you are talking with knowledge. If you think we should cover more people, you now have a handy rule of thumb to help you decide. That isn't bad. Think of all the issues that are dealt with by people yelling vague generalities at each other.

If you want to cover everyone who is without coverage, you now know that this would cost about $45.8 billion a year. There are other questions you might want to ask.

• Is this a lot for a government?
• Would it grow?

- Would it include just legal residents?
- Should mental health coverage be included?

Numbers do not answer these questions, but numbers elevate public policy discussions to a more rational level.

Are we spending defense dollars on the right things? As this is written, American soldiers in Iraq face the danger of death and injuries from roadside bombs. The military was not prepared for the roadside bombs in particular, but they developed vehicles that provide excellent blast protection.

The Cougar is a armored vehicle that comes in a couple of versions which are called Mine Protected Vehicle (MPV) or Mine Protected Ambush Resistant Vehicles (MARV). This exceptionally safe troop carrier comes in different versions such as the smaller Medium Mine Protected Vehicle or Cheetah, which is better for maneuvering an urban combat zone.[3] Its cousin is a Mine Protected Vehicle (MPV) known as the Buffalo. A buffalo can spot and disarm or destroy roadside bombs. The Buffalo has a twenty-five-foot arm that reaches out to examine suspicious objects by the road. If one of them goes boom, it does so too far from soldiers to cause damage.[4] These vehicles have been shown to work in tests and in action in Iraq. Should we then buy enough to cover all the roads that soldiers must drive? One consideration is cost. News reports say that it will cost $45.7 million for 122 vehicles. Dividing $45.7 million by 122 shows that a Cougar costs $374,590.

All the branches of the military are spending what we in Jersey call "bloody fortunes" on new, fancy, and very expensive weapons. The U.S. Air Force is currently buying F22A Raptors, the next generation in fighter jets. As of September 2006, these planes run about $137 million each, according to *Defense Industry Daily*.[5]

You may gasp, "WOW! Should we get the new fighter jet? What threatening enemy has anything approaching that fighter that we must match in technology? Or should we use that money for comparatively inexpensive armored vehicles for soldiers so they are not killed and maimed in their lightly armored trucks by explosive devices?" I think this is exactly what an aware and concerned citizen should say. There may be a good reason for spending this much for a fighter; as citizens we deserve to hear it, before we decide what weapons systems to buy. Yes, the military are the experts, but we are concerned citizens and those soldiers are our sons and daughters.

The *Wall Street Journal* won the Pulitzer Prize for a 1999 series of defense articles. One story asked the question: "Nuclear Arsenal Is Poised for War — Is It the Right One?"[6] Given events since 1999, that question was prescient and can easily be answered with today's hindsight. So what about now? Do we have enough nuclear weapons to deter sane countries from using them against us? If so, maybe we need to rethink priorities.

The *Journal* article tells the story of The Wyoming, an Ohio Class nuclear submarine with twenty-four nuclear tipped missiles. Each is a MIRV-type missile with eight warheads that can be targeted independently. That makes 182 nuclear strikes in one submarine. We have eighteen such submarines, for a total strike force of 3276 warheads. Is there any threat to the U.S. that could not be taken care of by one or two of these missiles? That doesn't include other types of missiles. Conceivably, we have reached the point at which we have enough.

The navy is spending billions each on a new aircraft carrier and billions more for planes for the carrier. Each carrier costs about $5 billion. We have eleven carriers and we are currently building more. No other potential enemy nation has even one full-sized aircraft carrier.[7] Against whom will we deploy these newest carriers? It might also be worth asking how many modern armored vehicles we could buy with the billions for a carrier and the billions for planes for the carrier, we are currently spending. Let us take the easy way out and just allocate one million dollars for each modern armored vehicle. This means that for every billion dollars we spend on an aircraft carrier, we can buy one thousand modern armored vehicles. It is your country and ultimately it is your choice. Don't be shy. It might even be your child in one of those vehicles. The old saying that wars are too important to be left to generals is probably true regarding military equipment.

A politician who cares a whit about our soldiers should raise a fuss about this misplaced priority so our soldiers could accomplish their mission and live to tell the tale. If you want to look further at numbers in this situation, you can Google Cougar and find that one of the less expensive Cougar models costs roughly $400,000 each. The Army would like to buy about eight thousand. Again, it seems like a lot of money.

But the military, as an article in *Popular Mechanics* notes, spends $10 billion a year for ballistic missile interceptors.[8] These interceptors were originally designed to stop Soviet missiles. Add this to $9 billion for a new generation jet designed to take on MIGs, $2 billion for a new strategic bomber, and the Navy plans to build seven new DD(X) Multi-Mission Destroyers for $4.7 billion each. The "multi-missions" of the DD(X) remain mysterious to many. It is supposed to take the place of the Spruance Class Destroyer and the Perry Class Frigate for carrier escort, antisubmarine warfare and naval support of ground troops. Perhaps you can justify some of this spending; perhaps not.

Here is another example of what I think is overkill. A short time ago we had 13 ballistic missile submarines (SSBNs) and we decided to build one more. The new submarines cost at least 2 billion dollars each. Each ballistic submarine carries 21 missiles. Each missile carries at least ten warheads, which can be independently targeted. Using a little arithmetic we can see that each submarine can destroy 210 targets. Do we even have enemies or potential enemies that have 210 targets worth one of our warheads? Even if we do, what are the other submarines for? Sure a few may get lost, confused, destroyed, or have the radio up too loud to heard the latest instructions, but we have thirteen. Meanwhile our soldiers are losing their limbs or dying because of a lack of proper equipment. An informed citizenry may have been of some help to our soldiers. Since few of us are going to war shouldn't we pay enough attention to be of help?

After doing the simple arithmetic, and barring other information that changes my thinking, I'm leaning toward buying the Cougars and Buffalos first.

Often, with a few simple arithmetic calculations, you can get a better understanding of government decisions and take a hard look at what you are hearing about them. Numbers don't always tell the whole story, but when it comes to public policy, one doesn't go far without bumping into them. Working the numbers, you have the knowledge to be more informed in answering the larger questions. A citizen who checks the facts and thinks through the numbers is less likely to be led astray.

Stanford University's conservative economist Thomas Sowell points to one academic journal that reported, "Every year since 1950, the number of American children gunned down has doubled." I cannot find the exact number of children killed by firearms in 1950. After working the numbers, though, I'm skeptical that this is so.

Even if you start out with just two children killed in 1950, by 1984 hundreds of million of children gun victims. In 2007 there were only 300 million people in the U.S.[9]

The Children's Defense Fund, which has an anti-firearms bias and would, if anything, over-report the figures, counted 2827 children's deaths from all gun-related violence in 2003. That's a lot, but it isn't 528 million.[10] Also, a number of these "children" are in the large, young adult category.

Count the police cost. Adding one new cop to the Los Angels Police Department costs an initial $60,000.[11] That is a good number for people of Los Angeles to use in assessing need versus resources and whether money ought to be allocated for more cops or more cop cars (or whatever). Keep in mind, of course that this initial expense is not all to consider. The new officer will cost more in salary and benefits as time goes by. Still you have some kind of a marker even when costs vary. This is comparable to the costs in police forces for other places. Whether you decide that you want to reduce or increase the costs, you are thinking in terms of benchmarks. You are thinking through policy, not just reacting.

In the mid-2000s, Medicare, the federal program that pays for medical care for the elderly, is growing at about 7 percent a year.[12] If the government absorbs about 45 percent of the cost, the economy must grow by 32 percent a year to cover it. Since the economy grows at about 3 percent a year in a good decade, this means big trouble. If cheap cures for everything are found, we will be okay.

Approaching the situation from another angle is equally depressing. The Congressional Budget Office predicts that Medicare benefits will go from a plump $374 billion to a really chubby $851 billion in 2017.[13]

Displaying the numbers in a single chart often gives perspective, and sometimes a chart can settle a question for all but the most fanatic. One chart in the October 18, 2006, *The New York Times* lays out the health care expenditure per person and the life expectancy at birth for a number of countries. Table 5.1 shows that the U.S. spends far more per person on health care but has less to show for it than even countries with government provided health care.

Unless conservatives are going to argue that life isn't everything, they must concede that it is possible to have what is sometimes called "socialized medicine" yet pay less while living longer. This might even be a very good thing. You could argue that things are different in North American culture. We would bankrupt the government because we are not wiling to wait, as do Europeans, for surgery and other health services. I think this is true, but how likely is it that the cost would double because of our poor discipline?

You might want to argue that government controlled health insurance would result in adding even more intrusive power to the government. This might be true, but I don't think such arguments will sway most people. Conservatives might be much better off voting to provide government insurance to the small portion of the population that doesn't have it, while demanding

Table 5.1. Cost of Health Care and Life Expectancy

Nation	Medical Cost per Person per Year	Life Expectancy
United States	$6,252	77.4 years
Switzerland	$4,211	81.2 years
France	$3,337	80.3 years
Germany	$3,290	78.6 years
Sweden	$3,005	80.6 years
Japan	$2,462	82.1 years

that illegal immigrants be removed before such a plan is put in place. Perhaps it could be said that we can take care of everyone who is a citizen but not the entire world.

Do you have a picture in your head that portrays poor and lower middle class getting a raw deal from the government? There is nothing like the flow of self-righteous blood flowing through the veins to get some people going in the morning. You have probably read reports of how the rich are getting away with income tax murder.

The wealthy may be getting by with a lot, and I personally believe that the rich should pay more. But when it comes to the question of who ends up getting the most return for their tax investment with the federal, state, and local governments, the numbers could alter those pictures in your head.

The Tax Foundation separated U.S. households evenly into five income groups and evaluated taxes and spending at all government levels to see who receives most from government spending. In 2004, according to the Tax Foundation, the group with the lowest income received $8.21 in total government spending for each dollar in taxes spent. Middle income households received back $1.30 in services for each tax dollar, and the highest-earning group received 41 cents for each dollar paid. Sixty percent of all Americans receive more from government spending that they pay in taxes.[14]

Chapter Six

History

We have looked at the importance of working the numbers. For me history is fascinating stuff. Even if you are not in this category of beings who find history this interesting, you might be interested in seeing how knowing history can make you more knowledgeable.

In the heat of the undocumented alien debate in the United States, the entire effort to put millions of illegal immigrants on the path to citizenship was derailed by a single number. In May 2006 the Comprehensive Immigration Reform Act of 2006, a compromise version of the Secure America and Orderly Immigration Act of 2005, was on the road to passage. The focus of the U.S. Congress was on the economic benefit to the nation.

Then a study of past immigration patterns, applied to a current cost analysis, was released by a reputable researcher, Robert Rector of the Heritage Foundation. The study showed that putting all of the illegal immigrants on the path to citizenship would have a net cost of $16 billion.[1]

In case anyone wanted to contest this fact, Rector added that indications from past immigration patterns show that there would be a massive increase in immigrants beyond the legalization of the 12 million then estimated to be in the U.S. Families of the 12 million would follow, bringing the anticipated total to 66 million immigrants over twenty years. The total cost, above taxes paid by the immigrants, would be $60 billion over that twenty-year period. These numbers, based strongly in the study of history, effectively ended the 2006 effort to allow those who had come illegally to stay if they met the financial and time requirements.

The provisions of the Constitution of the United States help prove the value of history. To a large degree, our constitution is a list of corrections of mistakes made throughout the history of Western civilization.

The writers of the constitution knew about all sorts of mistakes that had been made in the past. The founding fathers learned from personal experience and from reading history. The mistakes made by the founders of past nations made, had occurred in the past and the founders thought they could avoid them by a thorough reading of history.

By reading the history of the Roman Republic and the Roman Empire, the founders knew that one danger to a democratic republic could come when a successful general wanted to take over the government. So the U.S. Constitution places military rule under the president, a civilian. They knew how easily people could use torture from reading about its use in Europe, so torture is not allowed. They read about the dangers of direct democracy in ancient Greece, so we don't have direct democracy at the national level. We are a republic and we have representative democracy.

None of this was included by chance. It all comes from a careful study of history. The founders knew that rulers had often banned the common people from owning weapons. So they said, in the Second Amendment, that people had a right (and sometimes a duty) to bear arms. We live in different times from the world of the founding fathers, but it is very hard for a reader of history to miss their intentions. They saw the lesson of history that armed citizens were an ultimate guarantee of liberty. The truth of history is reflected in one scene in the feature film *Braveheart* (1995). The people line up against the king with a grab bag of hoes and sticks, and the king's men have all the latest stuff. It wasn't as if the peasants wanted to go to war with pitchforks and tiny shields. Rulers prevented them from arming. An armed citizenry could turn on its rulers. The writers of the Constitution wanted to take from government the power to disarm citizens.

Rulers often took people across the ocean to be tried in far-away London. When trials were moved far from home then people were alone at a time when they most needed their loved ones around them. It forced them to use a lawyer they did not know. It cost money. People could not do much to help in their own defense. It caused pain to their loved ones. The Constitution included rules by which a defendant could demand to be tried near where the crime was alleged to have been committed. This is good, unless of course you are a rotten person who has committed a despicable crime, and you do not want to be tried in the district where people were affected by it. Then you can ask to have the trial moved to somewhere else. The request may not be granted, but you can ask.

The founders knew how disturbing it could be to have soldiers quartered in private homes. The soldiers would make a mess, eat everything, and leer at their host's daughter. Not good. So we have a rule that soldiers are not to be quartered in anyone's house.

We can gain perspective on our current lives by looking back through history at similar problems, their causes and solutions. *It's Getting Better All the Time* presents the greatest trends of the twentieth century in colorful and easy-to-understand graphics.[2] This optimistic book by Stephen Moore and Julian Simon reports dramatic improvements in health, wealth and the alleviation of poverty, the welfare of children, education, the environment and other areas.

From history, you can learn that not that much in today's news is all that new.

Are you surprised about how slowly we are winning in Iraq? In Barbara Tuchman's *The Guns of August* about the beginning of World War I, we read: "A German officer leaving for the Western Front said he expected to take breakfast at the Café de la Paix in Paris by September 2, 1914 (The war started in August 1914.). Russian officers expected to be in Berlin about the same time . . . an officer of the Imperial Guard asked the opinion of the Czar's physician whether he should pack at once his full-dress uniform to wear for the entry into Berlin or leave it to be brought up by the next courier coming up to the front."[3]

From history we gain perspective on today's ideas and values. We know we are running out of energy resources because the experts tell us so—and they frequently have. Social scientist Stanley Jevons wrote in 1865 that industrial growth in England would end because there soon would be no more coal to fuel the growth. Just so no one would think there was an alternative to coal, he added, "We cannot long continue our present rate of progress, because we would soon run out of oil as well."[4]

The Ultimate Resource 2, by Julian Simon points out that since the ultimate resource is human courage, energy, and intelligence, which will never run out. The following predictions are quoted:

- 1885, U.S. Geological Survey; "Little or no chance for oil in California."
- 1914, U.S. Bureau of Mines. "Total future production limit of 5.7 billion barrels, perhaps a ten-year supply."
- 1939, U.S. Department of the Interior. "Reserves to last only thirteen years."
- 1951, U.S. Department of the Interior. "Reserves to last only thirteen years."

The "experts" aren't always wrong, but neither are they always right.[5]

History is not an infallible guide to what should be done, but it can provide help in making wise judgments. Unfortunately, it often does this by challenging our view of the past and present, forcing us to change our minds about "what everyone knows." This may be why control over the telling of history has been so hotly contested in academia, the media, and Hollywood. These are the people who have been downgrading the importance of objective historical fact, saying that the facts depend on the historian's perspective. To an extent that's true. The left massages and even changes historical fact in defining race, class, and gender. There is, of course, some truth regarding history that "where you stand depends on where you sit."

The problem comes when any set of factors is used as a background for looking at the shape of the past, present, or future. Race, class, and gender have an effect, but so do a thousand other factors. Here are some examples of how reading history can instantly transform your views of the world. The following examples are from *Ethnic America: A History* by Thomas Sowell. Many of the best examples come on the subject of race, partly because race has become one of the dogmatic historical categories.[6]

Do you think it is of vital importance that teachers resemble their students so students will feel comfortable, or perhaps perform better when they see an example of success? Sowell writes that two groups known for good performance in schools are Jews, whose first American teachers were mostly Irish, and Asians, who have had few Asian teachers when they first came to America. When Jews came from Eastern Europe and Asians came from the Pacific Rim, they were taught in English, not their native languages.

When Jews arrived in the United States in large numbers, starting in the late nineteenth century, primary grade classes often reached nearly ninety pupils per teacher. At the turn of the century, classes of sixty, with students three to a seat were not unusual. This does not mean that bigger classes are better, but it might mean that class size is not the crucial factor in determining academic performance. It is possible that other factors motivate effort and are more basic than the ones that are usually considered. Education experts continually change their ways of teaching. The children in their classes succeed or fail, though, based more upon home culture than new curricula. You do not have to have an advance degree to look through history at the family and peer-attitudes that made Jewish and Asian immigrants so successful.

Most people today probably think that those who came from North America and Europe were the world's most notorious slave traders and masters. Were white people the biggest slave traders? Sowell agrees with Susanne Everett (*The Slaves: an Illustrated History of the Monstrous Evil.*[7]), saying that "the massive commercial sales of Negro slaves began after the conquest of Northern Africa by the Arabs in the eighth century." Sowell adds that Arabs were notably cruel slave masters. He writes that "British explorer David Livingston had nightmares for weeks after witnessing the treatment of slaves by Arabs. . . . Slavery in Europe had died out over the centuries, when Africans were brought to Spain by Arab slave traders." Arabs were the primary slave traders and owners of slaves for centuries. Since the rise of Islam, Muslims have been responsible for the largest and best organized kidnapping and slavery industry. I first saw this documented in Everett's *The Slaves*. Muslims took more slaves from Black Africa than any other people group, under conditions that cause a higher percentage of death on the way, than any Europeans or Americans.

Is widespread ownership of private property related to freedom? It is closely related, according to Richard Pipes. In his historical study *Property and Freedom,* Pipes shows that there have been few times in human history in which freedom has existed without private property.[8] If you have doubts, you could just apply some comparative analysis and see if you can compile a list of countries that have freedom without also having private property rights.

Are you bothered by professors who talk about how violent modern man is and how peaceful primitive people were? Then read Lawrence H. Keeley's history of early warfare, *War before Civilization: the Myth of the Peaceful Savage* and learn that the "proportion of war casualties in primitive societies always exceeds that suffered by even the most bellicose or war-torn modern states."[9] History can teach us that many of the pictures of the world in our head are wrong.

This is depressing: Education doesn't seem to improve character at all. It may even hurt. There has existed within extreme and violent movements of the last few hundred years a plethora of educated people. They believe in the most ridiculous ideas and become mad or violent if anyone laughs. Read, for example, *Heaven on Earth: The Rise and Fall of Socialism,* a history of socialist fantasies by Joshua Muravchik or Alastair Hamilton's *The Appeal of Fascism: A Study of Intellectuals and Fascism, 1919–1945,* a who's who of artists and intellectuals who supported fascism in the Twentieth Century.[10] Muravchik's study is the basis for a Public Broadcasting Service miniseries. Hamilton's book contains the names of people whose work I admire, including W.B. Yeats and George Bernard Shaw, who were as ready to be duped as the rest of us.

Eugene Lyons in 1941 coined the name "Red decade" to describe the 1930s love affair with Bolshevik style communism. His book *The Red Decade: the Stalinist Penetration of America* was one of the first well-documented current events studies.[11] Lyons catalogs the foolish thinking exhibited by American intellectuals before World War II. The best and brightest echoed the thoughts of Josef Stalin and defended this mass murderer. They chanted slogans devised in Moscow in favor of Germany after the signing of the Nonaggression Pact, August 24, 1939. They chanted the opposite slogans devised in Moscow after Germany turned on the USSR and invaded on June 22, 1941. Fine newspapers and magazines like *The New York Times* and the *New Republic* explained away evidence of mass murder and torture. Writer Edmund Wilson, for example, issued an overwrought peon of praise that described Lenin's statue, "the right hand outstretched and in the eyes a look both piercing and genial, at once as if he were giving back to labor what it had made and inviting it to share for the first time in its heritage of human culture, and as if he were giving to humanity a whole a future of which for the first time they were to recognize themselves as the masters, the power to create without fear whatever they have minds to imagine."[12]

It was common to achieve a place of leadership in the elite Nazi Schutzstafel, or SS, if one had a Ph.D. Many Nazi leaders were products of the first-class German university system. These enlightened scholars turned their minds to engineering the Final Solution, designed to eradicate Jews, Gypsies, and any other group out of favor with the intelligentsia. Many history books look with amazement and fascination at how bright people founded or promoted the most violent and unreasoning of totalitarian systems.

You'll laugh, you'll cry, you'll want to slap an intellectual on the face while reading Richard Wolin's *The Seduction of Unreason: The Intellectual Romance with Fascism from Nietzsche to Postmodernism.* Similar studies include Stephanie Courtois, editor, *The Black Book of Communism: Crimes, Terror, and Repression;* Paul Hollander, *Political Pilgrims: Travels of Western Intellectuals to the Soviet Union, China, and Cuba;* and Raymond Aron, *The Opium of the Intellectuals.*[13]

So much for being impressed by men and women of ideas.

In history, one can see the pitfalls of the coming years. While I do not agree with some of his analysis, Niall Ferguson is worth hearing for his views on the costs of empire building. See *Colossus: The Rise and Fall of the American Empire.*[14]

You may want to change your mind about spending on the military after you read and feel the despair of soldiers who were without proper military equipment and mental, physical, and spiritual preparedness for combat. T. R. Fehrenbach in *This Kind of War: The Classic Korean War History* gives such details.[15] Once you read the story of "The Death of Company B," whose anti-tank rockets were so old and out of date that they bounced off of the North Korean tanks, you realize the importance of proper military equipment.

You won't find a cure for HIV-AIDS in Frank Ryan's *The Forgotten Plague: How the Battle Against Tuberculosis Was Won—and Lost.*[16] However, Ryan's work applies to the politics surrounding the battle against AIDS and the infighting among scientists. You are reminded that people dismissed as "panic mongers," may still be right. Strict application of the best procedures won the fight against tuberculosis, but the larger battle was lost when supervision of the correct measure became lax. What are those measures? That too can be learned, or at least you can see a starting point and not have to start from the beginning each time there is a setback. Ryan shows the good, the bad, and the ugly of the intersection of science, the media and bureaucracy that is inevitable in the modern world.

By reading such history, you can examine your judgments of current public policy decisions. History never repeats itself in exact detail, but similar problems do arise and thus history allows you to reflect your judgments off similar situations.

The problem with finding and reading wonderfully detailed stories is that they can be long and cover a lot of details. People are busy. It might be a good idea to find a historian you trust and then read what that historian says in articles and essays as well as books. That way you can get the benefit of their judgment in short bursts. Victor Davis Hanson and Niall Ferguson are two historians I admire who write well and often in short essays. Both have recently written about the role of the U.S. in the world. Hanson is the more optimistic about the future success of U.S. foreign policy. A good example of the work of Hanson is *An Autumn of War: What America Learned from September 11 and the War on Terrorism.*[17] As noted above, Ferguson has written *Colossus.*

Good writing does not mean bad history. Hanson often deals with war and terrorism in his latest works. Since the area of war and terrorism is a specialty in itself, it is a good idea to enlist someone like Hanson as a guide. His views certainly keep you awake: "The key ingredients for successful conclusions of wars being humiliation coupled with mercy; a true end to hostilities is impossible without both." He backs these words up with examples. To wrestle with ideas supporting or countering his examples makes you wiser.

I think that anyone planning to create nations in the Middle East can benefit from reading Ferguson's book about previous attempts at creating nations in this region of the world. We need to hear his doubts about whether the United States will "pay the price" before you can say you have honestly thought about the issue in a rational, rigorous manner. His description of Britain's empire-building in the Middle East is worth the price of the book. Yes, you may read one section of a book and then go on with your life. Ferguson's take on the Spanish American War objective to "liberate" the Philippines is hard to hear. However, it is a history we should know before and not after we venture abroad. It doesn't mean we should not engage in foreign lands but it does mean that we will be better off if we go after reading about previous foreign policy efforts.

It is often easier to stay calm and analyze current situations by reading about similar past situations. For example, reading about the Korean War in *This Kind of War* may be a more objective way of thinking through similar aspects of today's events than to struggle through the account of an ongoing conflict. Fehrenback introduces the argument that a nation needs "centurions," professional soldiers who will stay and fight on the far frontiers for as long as needed. He looks at the problems democracies have fighting "brush fire" wars, while succeeding magnificently in fighting crusades such as World War II. Both of these issues can be lifted from the 1950s to discussions of the War on Terror.

Fehrenbach comes to a difficult conclusion. He finds it necessary for . . .

> free, decent societies to continue to control their military forces, but to quit demanding from them impossible acquiescence to the liberal view toward life. A "modern" infantry may ride sky vehicles into combat, fire and sense its weapons through instrumentation, employ devices of frightening lethality . . . but it must also be old-fashioned enough to be iron-hard, poised for instant obedience, and prepared to die in the mud. . . . If liberal, decent societies cannot discipline themselves to do these things, they may have nothing to offer the world. They may not last long enough.[18]

Even where there are plentiful documentary films, more can be learned from reading a book about the Marines in the Pacific, such as Robert Leckie's *Strong Men Armed,* to get sense of the suffering endured by soldiers in a war.[19] There is terror, fear, confusion and even humor to be found during the fight for Guadalcanal. Often the only way to get the whole story is to read it.

Without such remembered details of human experience, we cannot understand the thoughts and actions of another place and time. What reasoning led President Harry Truman to order the dropping of atom bombs on industrial cities of Japan? No one who did not go through World War II can fully appreciate the moment, but the immersion in a period that is possible in a good historical account can help.

Interviews with survivors of the Bataan Death March have appeared over the years to give shocking details of the murderous abuse visited on the thousands of U.S. soldiers, Philippines homeland troops, and noncombatants who were forced to walk eighty-five miles in brutal conditions through the Bataan Peninsula. The pictures of men staving off thirst by sucking ground moisture that collected on the bottoms of their pants legs or falling under random bayonet attacks are horrifying. Historical fact alone does not do justice to the self-sacrificing loyalty of men who risked their lives to steal eggs for a malaria stricken soldier near death.

After reading these events, you will be among those who remember the islands where so many died. Nothing can substitute for the dense details that can be presented in a book.

It helps to just see the facts in print. We do not need the inspiration of a painting showing George Washington standing in a long boat crossing the Delaware River. The facts of the Battle of Trenton on December 26, 1776, which restored the morale of Washington's army, are inspiring enough. W. Thomas Smith, Jr., a veteran who researched the battle, writes,

> The river—swollen and swift moving—was full of wide, thick sheets of solid ice. And unlike the romanticized portrayal of the operation in the famous painting by Emanuel Leutze (the one with Washington standing in his dramatic, martial pose, his determined face turned toward the far side of the river), the actual crossing was made in the dead of night, in a gale-like wind and a blinding sleet and snowstorm. Odds are, Washington would have been hunkered down in one of the 66-ft-long wooden boats, draped in his cloak, stoically enduring the bitter cold with his soldiers, some of whom were rowing or poling the boats against the ice and the current. . . .
>
> The soldiers were not properly outfitted for extreme winter conditions: Clothing was spare. Many men were in rags, some "naked," according to Washington's own account. Most had broken shoes or no shoes at all. . . .
>
> Back and forth throughout the night and into the wee hours of the 26th, the boat crews ferried the little army, a few horses, and 18 cannon across the Delaware. The crossing was complete by 4 a.m., but two hours behind schedule, and the temperatures were plummeting. At least two men, exhausted and falling asleep in the snow, froze to death.[20]

Such stories in themselves do not necessarily make one a more knowledgeable citizen, but they help form our understanding. Knowledge of historical context prepares one to better understand today's world. Keep in mind that the above historians are people I like. Find your own list. It is no harder than sorting out your friends from all the millions of people out there.

Chapter Seven

Double Standards

The use of double standards makes is easier for someone to win the contest of ideas. If we are held to lower standards than our opponents then our task is made easier.

People often use different standards to judge people they like and people they don't like. This is human nature. We tend to judge our loved ones differently than we judge others. If this isn't true for you, you might want to consider getting different loved ones. Certainly we would be disappointed if our mother didn't value us more highly than she does strangers.

When we are thinking about public issues, however, we want to be more objective. Most times we use a double standard without giving it a second thought, so it is necessary to make the effort to recognize double standard thinking. In the past, black people were judged by a much harsher standard than white people. Some would say that whites today are judged by a harsher standard. What do you think? Your judgment counts. Ultimately it will determine policy. My view is that there is just one group that should have the benefit of a double standard?American Blacks. That is, people who have black skin and whose families have been in this country for over two hundred years should be given extra help to get them to where they would be if we hadn't been wearing them out over the last few hundred years. I think that their suffering in this country warrants some special help. You need to decide for yourself.

U.S. foreign policy provides a large number of examples where we must make judgments regarding out public policies. One special area of deciding what standards to use, come about when we see the use of moral equivalence. Some people feel that when we talk about the deaths we cause in Iraq and the deaths caused by suicide bombers, we are talking about the same thing. Others think that this is unfair, since we are not trying to cause death to innocents and the Muslim fanatics are trying to kill innocents. Many people who attack the U.S. think that we are no better than our enemies. Those who defend the U.S. think that to equate the deaths we cause, with the deaths the suicide bombers cause, is like equating the deaths our soldiers caused during WWII, with the deaths caused by the Nazi soldiers during World War II, and they don't like this.

Neither do I.

You must evaluate the morality of national actions for yourself. Should a line of moral equivalence be drawn between the violence of the one who victimizes and the violent response of the victim? Should the actions of the attacker and the attacked be judged the same way? I don't think so. If it were, this gives a great advantage to the aggressor.

If you need examples of this way of assessing blame, read the news reports on Israel. Examples of moral equivalence abound. One article, "The Maimed," sympathized with those "who just happened to be in the wrong place in the Israeli-Palestinian conflict." These include Kinneret Boosany, a former waitress whose terrible injuries in a restaurant bombing have made her an international spokeswoman for peace. The article also has pictures and stories of other Israelis and Palestinians who have been maimed. The author's objectivity came into question when he equated the anguish of families of the bombing victims with the grief of the families of the murderous bombers. The article concludes with the idea that "to consider them is to be reminded not just of human cruelty and human stupidity [but also of] . . . human tenacity."[1] The reporter is so overwhelmed that he can't seem to differentiate between those who kill intentionally and those who are victims of those who kill intentionally.

Moral equivalence often works to the detriment of Israel, which often seems to be singled out for condemnation. Israelis are expected to absorb attacks without responding. If they do fight back, they are frequently accused of the "crossing of a red line" (Cable News Network) or "drawing additional countries directly into its intractable conflict" (*The New York Times*) or engaging in a "tit-for-tat" (*Pittsburg Post Gazette*). They are warned that retaliation "could aggravate anti-U.S. feelings in the region" or "destabilize a whole region" (*USA Today*). Were I a cynic, I would say that much of the planet has not reconciled itself to the fact that Jews have the ability to strike back at those who harm them.

World leaders often criticize the actions of African whites, particularly during the past colonial period the period of apartheid in South Africa. Whites certainly warrant some criticism, past and present, but is there reluctance to put brutal actions by black leaders against black Africans under the moral lens? Little is said about blacks killing blacks until a genocidal war has been underway for years.

Slavery still is practiced in Africa. The slave owners are invariably Muslim Arabs. The enslaved are almost always black Africans. Do you hear much about this situation? There is sporadic attention in the media on the slavery problem, but not many off the continent are even vaguely aware of it. The situation would seem to warrant the kind of outcry that would ensue if white South Africans owned their black neighbors. The evil is just as great, whether the slave holders and the enslaved are white, black, or of some other race and ethnicity. But it does make a difference who is oppressing whom when it comes to deciding whether to put a situation on the front burner. At this point, there seems to be little enthusiasm among the media for yelling at non-white, non-Christian, non-Westerners. Is there a double standard at work here?

Terms used can set up a double-standard. The term fetus refers to a developing child in the womb. However, in the abortion debate, fetus often is re-defined as something not yet human. In a March 19, 1999, letter to the editor of the *Home News Tribune,* a New Jersey paper, an observant reader named Irene Lenahan berated the editorial staff for an editorial headlined "Exclude pregnancy from Medicaid cuts." She asks, "How come when you write about abortion, you refer to an unborn baby as a fetus and you make it very plain you do not consider it murder to eliminate this fetus by having an abortion. When you champion prenatal care for illegal immigrants, all of a sudden it is an 'unborn baby.' Why is it not an unborn baby when abortion is concerned? Could it be you then would have to acknowledge that abortion is the murder of this unborn child?"

I say the lady has a point I suspect the editorial staff has been using a double standard so frequently that their word choice dehumanizes the unborn and does so without conscious effort.

When Clarence Thomas, a conservative judge, was nominated to be on the Supreme Court, feminists stormed up to the U.S. Senate on behalf of Anita Hill, a woman who charged that Thomas had made unwanted sexual advances to her. Some in the media found it noteworthy that feminists couldn't get out of bed to mention Paula Jones, a woman who claimed to have been similarly treated by a powerful man named Bill Clinton. About the discrepancy was pointed out, the leader of the stormers, U.S. Representative Patricia Hill, said in a "reluctant telephone interview" that "People are busy. They have only so many hours to breathe. People just don't rally every day. They eat. They work."[2] Was she saying that there wasn't a double standard; the poor woman is exhausted.

To avoid being taken in by double-standard arguments, be sure to ask yourself whether the levels of details are the same. Often in colleges today, the flaws of the West, and especially the United States, are examined in excruciating details while the better aspects of this country are barely mentioned. If your view of the United States was determined by college books and college professors would your relatives have even wanted to come here?

Double standards can also be achieved by leaving some things out. Topper Garnet wrote an influential book, which led to stories in *People* magazine and other publications, "Ten Wonder Women of the '80s." On the "wonder woman list" was Jane Fonda, with much positive comment, but nothing about her rather prominent role in the anti-Vietnam War movement.[3] She repeatedly went to North Vietnam to encourage the North Vietnamese Communists, and met with the American prisoners of war, some of whom were tortured because they refused to meet with her. She had photos taken at an anti-aircraft gun that was used to kill American pilots. None of those shining moments in Fonda's life were mentioned in the coverage I saw.

Pictures often play a key role in setting up a double standard because it turns out that a picture often really is worth a thousand words. When stills and action footage are shown in any media format, the emotions are open to manipulation. That may be appropriate or not, but it is something to keep in mind as a news consumer. It is fair to use pictures and details for both sides of an argument. If I mention the plight of the slaves in modern day Africa, the words have more impact if you look directly at a slave named Mbarek in *Newsweek* magazine. It is one thing to talk about soldiers being maimed in Iraq. It is another matter to look at the pictures in the February 15, 2002, issue of *The New York Times* magazine that show a soldier holding his wife, and you can see that the arm around her ends at the soldier's elbow.

Chapter Eight

The Media

It is just the human situation that we have only so much time and emotional resources to deal with problems. We need someone or something to cut down on the potential material. The media filters out some material and helps determine what we will think about from all the potential happenings and facts in the world. The media sets our mental agenda.

Unfortunately they often display a pack mentality. One media personality gets excited about some subject or takes a position. Soon other media people are doing the same thing. If you were listening to the mainstream media reports from another planet, what disease would you think was killing the most people? You would probably think AIDS and you would be wrong.

There is truth to the frequently heard statement that political reality becomes real only after it appears on television. What has been happening in Somalia? Are the people still starving in Somalia, or being brutalized in Haiti? Who knows? If it isn't on television, who worries about it?

Each year at the anniversaries of the atomic bomb attacks on Hiroshima (August 6, 1945) and Nagasaki (August 9, 1945), there is some news report about the tragedy of using the atomic bomb and how it might not have been necessary. Occasionally I have seen articles stating that white people bombed people of color. Soon after, a professor is quoted as demanding that we all apologize for the bombing. Where is the context?

What if the media began its story by asking how many Japanese lost their lives during the bombing, how many Japanese gave their lives in total during the conflict, and how many people died at the hands of the military organization supported by the industries in Hiroshima and Nagasaki? If you took the "What Everybody 'Knows'" quiz at the start of this book, you know the answers.

The media plays a role by just keeping us focused on particular events and not others. On August 1, 2005, *Time* magazine used "Hiroshima at 60" as its cover story. The cover picture was about a women who had lost her entire family on the day the atomic bomb was dropped on Hiroshima. Three pages of photos showed the terrible effects of radiation on survivors. Twelve pages were devoted to the story. That included a one-page essay on the morality of dropping the bombs. Little space was given to those who think the attacks were morally appropriate and strategically warranted. The essay on morality concludes, "The discomforting truth is that the Allied leaders strode unhesitatingly into the atomic age."

This is not to heap yet more blame on the Japanese for what the government of their great-grandparents wrought. But we do need perspective if the media are going to lay guilt at the feet of President Harry Truman and the United States. About 140,000 are estimated to have died because of the Hiroshima bombing and 74,000 because of the bombing of Nagasaki. About 20 million people were killed by the Japanese. More than is usual for wartime were simply murdered rather than killed in military engagements. Occupation forces staged beheading contests in China and conducted experiments on innocents using poison gas and biological agents. Women were forced into prostitution to serve the soldiers. Japanese doctors frequently performed experiments on living patients including a dissecting people while they were alive.

The torture and cruelty against Chinese civilians was horrific, but this side is seldom mentioned by the media when it comes to looking for the motivation for such destruction. My thought is that, as a news consumer, I can appreciate the horrors afflicted in the bombings while understanding what brought on this suffering. More thoughtful coverage would put the news into its context.

The America media has specialized in making icons of suffering non-Western, non-white peoples since the 1960s. It is as if one movie plays on an endless loop.

As Ben Shapiro, the author of *Brainwashed: How Universities Indoctrinate America's Youth,* has noted, moral equivalence is a widespread disease.[1] He cites Paul Erlich, a professor of population studies at Stanford, who compared the Holocaust to the dropping of the atom bomb on Japan. "To compare the slaughter of 6 million innocents with a military action that saved hundreds of thousands of lives is reprehensible," says Shapiro. I heartily agree.

We have already mentioned the problem of moral equivalence. Many a woman would be pleased if a lover had half the passion for them as mainstream media has for moral equivalency regarding the war against Islamist terrorism. In every other war we have been pleased to announce who the enemy is; sometimes labeling said enemy with slurs, such as Hun or Jap. We were never afraid of what the enemy would think about us if we used a derogatory term. We thought more about what we were going to do to them than about what they were going to think of us. We even relished the idea of killing huge numbers of them and rejoiced when we did so. This was because we thought that we were very good and they were very bad.

Nowadays a fair slice of the media and academic community are unsure that we are good and the terrorists are bad. They are more comfortable with moral equivalence than with thinking about us being really, really right and our enemies as really, really wrong. This belief in moral equivalence can be seen when reporters implicitly or explicitly report our sins (e.g. Abu Ghraib) as being on a par with theirs (e.g. killing sixty civilians in a Baghdad market on July 2, 2006). Indeed, at moral equivalence central, *The New York Times,* our sins warrant more space, in more prominent places, than their sins.

I sometimes wonder how the experts who believed in the moral equivalence of the two sides in World War II would have won that war. Actually, the left did take that approach during the first part of the war in Europe. The left equated the class society of England with the "problems" the Soviet Union was encountering internally and externally. It was not until Nazi Germany attacked the Soviet Union that the left came alive with enthusiasm for war.

In that June 17, 2006, editorial, *The New York Times* expressed the agony of wrestling with the problem of bringing peace to the Middle East. The editorial writer made such comments as "Armed thugs from Fatah are fighting it out with armed thugs from Hamas. Israel is building unilateral fences and defining borders. If the two sides do not really want to negotiate with each other, the argument goes, there's nothing much outsiders can do to help." Also noted was the following: "Already, rockets are raining down again on innocent Israeli and Palestinians civilians, inflaming passions on both sides."

If you want to see what is wrong here, transfer this language to the events of 1942. If the year was 1942 and *The Times* said "If Germany and the United States do not really want to negotiate with each other, the argument goes, there's nothing much outsiders can do to help. . . . Already, rockets are raining down on Russians in Stalingrad and German civilians in Berlin, inflaming passions on both sides" would that sound right to you?

Is there something about moral equivalence that actually causes and sustains wars? Yes, there is. To engage in moral equivalence is to encourage the aggressor.

The New York Times has a special place in any discussion of the role of the media in America. It is the newspaper of record for this planet in general and the United States in particular. Even William F. Buckley, Jr., the conservative journalist and educator, has said that *The Times* has become as important to all of us as our arms and legs. In addition to being the newspaper of record, *The Times* is the fountainhead—the beginning and end of all legitimate liberal opinion in America. Liberals may champion causes that this newspaper does not care about, but few causes not championed by the editors will succeed. Few leading liberals will start a crusade without the backing of *The Times.*

While this publication seems to be more and more dogmatic, it has to somehow maintain its reputation as the objective newspaper of record. Therefore, you can find many facts in *The Times* that go against its worldview. Stories it doesn't like may be buried in the back pages, but those stories are there. The facts that matter may be buried, and they may be at complete odds with the headline. They will, however, be somewhere in the story.

Finding these facts has become a bit of an indoor sport for those who naturally prefer the indoors. This is good news if you are strapped for funds and can only afford one paper. It is also fun to quote from *The New York Times* in a debate, hoisting your opposition on their own petard, even if the petard requires patience and a keen eye to discover.

The Times seems to be very much in favor of open borders. At least they seem to think that reducing the percentage of whites is always a good thing. Or, maybe it suits them to aggravate the mass of Americans. For whatever reason, the newspaper has done its best to support any easing of immigration, and it has more stories on the virtues of various immigrants than there are grains of sand on the Atlantic coast.

One of the basic arguments against easy immigration and amnesty is that immigrants will take jobs and reduce pay rates for working Americans. In one edition of *The Times,* on page 16, far from the front page and just as far from the editorial page, is an article with the headline "Study Sees Increase in Illegal Hispanic Workers in New Orleans."[2] So far, it is possible that the Hispanic workers have come more for relaxation and jazz than for work itself. Sadly, the story says that "About a quarter of the construction workers rebuilding New Orleans are illegal immigrants, who are getting lower pay, less medical care, and less safety equipment than legal workers, according to a new study by professors at Tulane University and the University of California, Berkeley."[3] Isn't this at least some evidence that illegal immigrants do drive down wages and reduce medical care benefits?

The practice of including but burying the facts that harm the newspaper's causes is fun to hunt for. *The Times* is like Ragu®, the fine Italian style spaghetti sauce that advertises, regarding its many fine ingredients, that "it's all in there."

One area where the media exercises a kind of invisible control is in its choice of images. Like a good detective story, often the key to solving the mystery is something that is not mentioned or noticed. One recent example can be seen in the outbreak of stories about a murderer who came off as a very sympathetic character if you read most of the stories about him. You would have sympathized less had you followed your Internet search engine to photos of the victims of Stanley "Tookie" Williams. Williams was the co-founder of a violent gang called the Cripps. He had murdered a number of people himself, mainly by using a shotgun at close range. Tookie was eventually sentenced to death for killing some of those people during various robberies.[4]

On death row, he wrote an autobiography, and a movie was made about his life. He claimed to have changed completely. He wrote books for children gave interviews to help children and gave talks via television hookups designed to prevent violence by young people. In 2005, as the time for his execution drew near, the media ran a flurry of stories and opinion pieces about Tookie. A small army of supporters worked feverishly to save him from execution.

None of the stories I saw mentioned the names of the people who had been murdered by Williams. None gave details of their lives. It was strange, but ordinary, that details of the murderer's life were vented in full while the victims seemed to vanish into thin air. Did one victim, Albert Owens, for example, have any children? Was he a veteran? Did he like sports? What about Tsai-Shay Hang, Yen-I Yang or Yee-Chen Lin, who were killed during a robbery of their family-owned motel? Which among them were married? Did they have any hobbies or did work consume most of their waking hours? Did they relax by playing cards or by watching television? How long had the family saved before they had the money to buy the hotel? What were their long-term goals? I don't know. Like so many victims before and since, they just seemed to disappear as human beings full of hopes and dreams.[5]

Because of the Internet, it is now possible to find out details about the victims and snatch them back from the thin air in which so many victims seem to go. Are victims often not portrayed in detail to garner more sympathy for the criminals? This goes along with the worldview of the left that America is fundamentally evil. If someone did something wrong, the natural suspect is our society and its lack of governmental efforts to help those in need. This worldview allows none but the unsophisticated masses to say that the underlying cause of Tookie Williams's crimes was Tookie. Those who feel that there is something wrong with the very foundations of the U.S. blame poverty, racism, or neglect by society. Those who think that the fundamental cause of the murders lay in Tookie's own cruel heart are often thought to be at best naïve and, at worse, racist.

A nice thing about the Internet as an alternative news medium is that a person can look more deeply into events in the news at home. Since there is easy access, many people use it to post useful information. Friends of the victims of crime can now reclaim their sons, daughters, or friends and make them people you might care about. In the case of Williams, someone found and posting pictures of the victims after Tookie had shot them at close range with a shotgun, a weapon designed to hit a person with a wide pattern of BB-sized projectiles. Instead of a small entry hole, there is a fairly wide blotch of ripped open flesh that looks ugly and raw. Looking at these images, descriptions of the wounds, biographies of the victims, and descriptions of the emotions of grieving relatives and friends, one had a good deal less sympathy for their killer.

My guess is that this is exactly why the mainstream media do not include such words or images for that very reason.

People are not aware of the impact of the media is in regard to the use of details. The impact of a story can be easily altered by including or omitting telltale details. In many of the texts and materials used in college today, the details of the faults of the West, and of America in particular, are discussed in "loving detail" while the faults of other countries are often left out.

But if you want to be a citizen gone wild, consider the details on one side. Then to be fair, consider the details from both sides.

Look at how easily the details can move our emotions. Eric Dash did so in a *New York Times* Business Section story, "Off to the Races Again, Leaving Many Behind," about executive pay.[6] If you want to have good days, just read the headline and go about your business. If you want to risk turning into an instant Marxist, read the details.

The business story starts with the news that James P. Smith started ConAgra Foods in 1977, earning $6.40 an hour. Thirty years later, Smith earned $13.25 an hour, for a total of $28,000 a year. He lamented that he will probably never be able to retire and have enough to live on. Next, the story talks about the chief executive of ConAgra, Bruce Rhode, who has been able to retire on the $45 million he made during his eight years at ConAgra and his retirement package worth $20 million. Why Bruce couldn't save enough from the $45 million was not made clear. You may say that the man did a fine job and thus deserves every dime he gets.[7]

The thing is, during the time Rhode was in charge, the company's share price fell 28 percent. Sadly, the company had to cut nine thousand jobs. Accounting problems surfaced frequently during his years at the company. This is a good example of how details make emotional impact. Contrast the above story with other facts in the story. For example, in 1940, half of all corporate executives earned more than fifty-six times the average pay, and in 2004 half of all executives earned more than 104 times the average worker's pay.[8] This is bad, but when I read about Rhode and Smith, I am ready to hit someone—perhaps Rhode.

I think that there is such a thing as the mainstream media and I think that they have a rather intense point of view which they cling to in ways that teenage boys and girls can only dream of, and that you often need a powerful way to dislodge those dogmatic positions that they hold with religious zeal. Being aware that this is done may help.

Chapter Nine

Solutions or Trade-offs?

Should we view public policy as problems for which there are solutions, or should we say that only some public policy problems have solutions? Should we ask if the problems have a government solution? Perhaps many problems really have trade-offs and we should look at those trade-offs before we decide on a solution.

What would a person who views a world full of solutions say in regard to . . .

- public-funded education for the children of illegal immigrants?
- bad housing?
- prisons for young offenders?
- increasing defense spending?
- affirmative action for women?

What are the possible answers? Is there a solution? What are the tradeoffs and costs?

Very few public problems have solutions that are without substantial cost. Sometimes you can only trade one consequence for another. Not all public policy issues involve good guys and bad guys.

Can we take care of all medical problems and still keep costs down? If so, how?

The government can provide medical care for everyone, but this is very hard to do while controlling costs. Nations in which the government provides medical care for everyone usually deal with cost by forcing people to wait for elective surgery. They avoid spending money for inefficient medical care, including such things as renal dialysis for the elderly, taking heroic measures to save premature babies, and allowing a new mother more than a one-day stay in the hospital after giving birth.

Often policy decisions are made for emotional reasons. What if we want to add a rational approach? What if we want you to consider the costs as well as the benefits of a policy? This is important, but the media often treats policy choices as one big soap opera where the only choice is that of being a good person or a bad person. You are either for helping people rebuild where they live after a natural disaster or you are a bad person. The possibility of another approach, for example, helping people move to a safer area, is rarely mentioned.

In real life, it is very rare to have a program without cost. The question for an educated, rational person is, "Do the costs outweigh the benefits?"

A federal government program helps people after their property has been destroyed by a natural disaster. This is good, but it may eventually have a poor result. Since victims of natural disasters can count on cash grants, federally subsidized flood insurance and low-interest loans to bail them out, they may build in areas they would avoid if the federal government were not there to rescue them.

In the past five years, the federal government has spent about $62.3 billion in flood relief. This is three times what the government paid during the previous ten years, according to the House of Representatives Joint Economic Committee in 2006.[1]

Topsail Island, North Carolina, is a twenty-three-mile-long spit of land no more than half a mile across at its widest point. Three times in two years, it was flooded by hurricanes. Each time, the federal government paid to rebuild the damaged houses. Without federal aid, life on the island would almost be impossible. People live here because the federal government subsidizes the insurance. People pay $300 to $500 in annual premiums, but the insurance would be non-existent or many times more expensive if not for the federal government.[2]

Typical is Ms. Sullivan, who bought her home there in the early 1990s. It has eight bedrooms and five baths. After one hurricane, Sullivan collected $411,000 in federal funds to repair the damage. Two months later, another hurricane came through. The federal government provided $4.134 million in insurance payments and grants. She received $4.115 million in low-interest loans from the Small Business Administration. She bought a new home that had wind and flood damage from Hurricane Debbie. She says, "I wouldn't have bought again without flood insurance."

In other areas, homes are constructed on flood plains (which are called that because. . . .) and mudslide-prone hills.

European countries tend to have greater job security than in the U.S., but in the U.S. there is a lower unemployment rate. These points may be related since companies are more reluctant to provide jobs where it is harder to fire someone who is not doing the job or is no longer needed. Some multinational firms actually choose to build factories in the U.S. where it is easier to fire people. This is one of the reasons Toyota and BMW built North American plants.

People often speak of solutions, instead of trade-offs or costs when they are trying to influence the public, especially when they are running for office. It is an easy way to make the other side appear to lack compassion.

It is easy to say that we should make the drug companies supply drugs at low costs. What might be the benefit of such a program? What might be the costs? Will there be less money available to create new drugs? How much of the high cost of one drug goes for research on a new drug? Surely such questions need to be answered before we take sides. Is it worthwhile?

When people are running for office they often offer to bring benefits to the voter. That is nice. There is often no profit in it for them to point out that with the benefits come costs, perhaps obvious, perhaps not. Few voters like costs. Fewer will vote for someone who points out the costs. So it is incumbent on you, the righteous citizen, to ask "Is there a cost?" Do not be overly concerned. If you don't like the cost; you can just ignore it.

Most articles about costs are dull and no fun at all. There are exceptions, like a column by Paul Mulshine that appeared in the Newark, New Jersey, *Star-Ledger,* "A surfer dude's plan for reform." Mulshine tells you the cost of some of the most popular government regulations, those meant to protect the environment. Particularly the column is about the manufacturer who created foam blanks that could be shaped into surfboards, snowboard, and skateboards. Gordon "Grubby" Clark was going out of business because, as he saw it, "the regulators would much rather threaten a citizen with fines and jail time than find a simple solution to a simple problem." He claims that "You could build . . . facilities outside of the United States for the cost of permits in California."[3]

I am neither a surfer dude, nor an expert in California environmental regulations, but I think that, after looking at the cost-benefit ratios of some government regulations, one could find laws that could be changed to greatly aid economic health without serious harm to the environment.

Surprises are so frequent in public policies that they have there own name—unintended consequences. Here is one in *The New York Times,* "Exchanging Cigarettes for Bagels."[4] According to this article, a fair number of public health specialists think Americans may have traded one bad habit for another in the campaign to stop smoking. The evidence is substantial. According to David Williamson of the Center for Disease Control and Prevention, Americans gained twenty pounds from 1980 to 2000. This was a reversal of a twenty-year trend. Dr. Williamson thinks that the decline in cigarette smoking led to the enormous weight gain. It appears that American need something to soothe themselves and if they lose one vice they will switch to another. Cigarettes are still more deadly than the dreaded jelly donuts, but it does give new meaning to the saying "There's no such thing as a free lunch."

Chapter Ten

Apples and Oranges

Are you comparing things that should not be compared? People often use inappropriate comparisons, unconsciously or to construct a cheap argument for their view.

Let us say that you want to convince people that there is widespread discrimination against non-white groups in the U.S. Some years ago I saw a report on the U.S. poverty rate in 2000. The report said that the rate was at its lowest point in twenty years. However, there was a large gap between the median annual income of $44,000 and the Hispanic household median annual income of about $28,000.

Such statistics are often given as evidence that the economic playing field is still uneven. Indeed this is often done. The story on the incomes of different races on the MSNBC Web site is typical, speaking of black-white "gaps."[1] This and so many other articles imply that the gap is due to racial prejudice.

However, there might be other reasons for the gap.

First, the longer people have been in this country, the better they do economically. Many Hispanics are recent arrivals. The longer they are here, the better they will do. Generally, this is true of all immigrants. This obviously is one of the reasons that people come to America. It is not by itself evidence of racial bias.

Second, the higher the education, the greater the earning potential; this is according to U.S. Census Bureau statistics for 2005. People come to America so that their children will be better educated than they are. I hear people talk about how minority students don't always graduate from high school. Neither of my parents got into high school. Of their three children, two have Ph.D.s and one has a Master's Degree. If it is true that recent arrivals are less educated than natives, it might be that immigrants still view America as the place to come to get a better education, not a place of bias.

Third, less educated poor people tend to have larger families than middle-class educated people. Well-educated people have fewer children. A good example is professors. Professors profess to love children, protect children, put children first, and advocate for children. But they don't have a lot of children themselves. Perhaps this is done so there will be room for other people's children. Hispanics, who tend to arrive poor and less educated than native-born Americans, will soon enough have smaller families. Seldom do you see a large second- or third-generation family in any ethnic group? Smaller families tend to be richer families. How many self-earned billionaires have a gaggle of children?

Fourth, immigrants tend to have more children and have them at a younger age. This hurts their chances of making more money, especially those who have children out of wedlock or drop out of school to take care of the children. This happens more often with immigrants than it does with people whose families have been in the country longer. If a parent is taking care of the children instead of working, that family earns less than a family with two people working. If one parent drops out of school to take care of the children, earning potential is lower than in families in which everyone stays in school.

Fifth, immigrants often lack a good command of the English language. Having good English skill is necessary for gaining a well-paying job.

Sixth, some cultures greatly value the entrepreneurship skills needed to start small businesses. The two best ways of moving into the middle class are through education and owning a business. Make a list of groups that are doing well economically. How many of these groups have a tendency to own their own businesses?

People like to compare apples and oranges because it is an easy thing to do. It is often used in discussing emotional subjects. Today that may well mean areas involving race or gender.

You can often see a statistic that says women earn a certain percentage of what men earn or that blacks earn a certain percentage of what whites earn. But when you see these figures, ask if other factors might cause the difference.

Often the trick with apples-to-oranges comparisons is to use averages that disguise the fact that if you were more precise you would not be able to prove your ideological point. In some cases, a single factor that is not included will account for most or all of the differences. In the case of a comparison between men and women, there is often an attempt to show bigotry where little or none exists.

With male-female pay disparities, one significant difference is continuous work experience. The greater the period of continuous work experience, the higher the salary. Since women are more likely to take time off for children they often have less continuous work experience. There still might be an element of prejudice, but unless you make sure that you are comparing apples and apples, you are not making an honest comparison. You can argue that society does not do enough to help women with children, but this is another matter. The relevant question is, How do women who don't take time off to have children fare in pay disparity?

Chapter Eleven

Language

Does language cloud an objective view? One easy way to gain an advantage in an argument is to use words that are seemingly objective but sneak in a negative impact.

While discussing economic systems, someone uses the word capitalism, a term that has negative connotations for many people. For these people, a capitalist is mean-spirited and doesn't care about the poor, practicing discrimination if it helps the bottom line.

To see whether a word seems negative or positive, think, "Would I care if that word was applied to me? Would I like to be called a . . . capitalist?

People who like capitalism would probably choose to use a term like free enterprise. They would probably choose to point out that capitalism is just freedom in the economic sphere, with all the benefits and costs of freedom. Those who think this is the best system would likely emphasize that countries that have a good deal of freedom in the economic sphere are much richer than other countries, have a larger middle class, allow the poor to rise to the middle class, and in general accept others, regardless of race, gender, ethnicity, or place of origin. While not all free enterprise countries are free; all free countries have free enterprise.

An article in the *Wall Street Journal* was headlined, "The Supreme Court Can End the Charade."[1] By using the word charade the writer has taken a stand. In this case the article was an essay on the editorial pages, so use of the loaded word was entirely appropriate.

When an article in the same issue talks about "Canada's extravagant welfare system," we conclude that we should seek another article to find a positive view of the Canadian welfare system. People who think that the government should help people in need might not like to use the word welfare, which smells like people who aren't doing too much to get their money. Again, test out words by applying them to yourself. Imagine your father telling your mother, "Great news. Alice's fiancé is now getting welfare." Would you feel better or worse upon hearing those words?

Here are some handy examples of words that attempt to end an argument before it starts by labeling those on one side as bad people:

- *Extremist.* Those on the left tend to use this term more frequently of those on the right than the other way around. An "extremist" is so totally out of logical and reasonable argument that they are too embarrassed to even attempt to argue their case because they suspect people may break into public laughter upon hearing their arguments. No one in the mainstream media has ever met a liberal extremist. Not even politicians who compare our soldiers to Nazis warrant the label.
- *Wedge Issue.* Issues held by conservatives that for some reason become troublesomely popular. Currently, the best example is illegal immigration; +other wedge issues include gay marriage and affirmative action.
- *Maverick.* Mavericks are Republicans who are willing to buck the party to promote liberal views. The term never refers to Democrats who hold conservative views.

Biased language doesn't necessarily mean that the argument is flawed. You should just be aware that if the writer calls someone a fascist, they probably have an intense point of view, even if the person referred to actually is indeed a fascist.

Here are some examples of frequently used words that indicate a point of view and probably a lack of objectivity:

Loaded words are charged with hidden meaning. If someone calls you stupid or reactionary, they probably don't like you or your views. If they call you patriotic, they probably do like you. One frequently hears the word *wing.* It is one thing to say, "I love buffalo wings drenched in blue cheese." But when used to describe political views, the term means something else, a partisan bloc.

People identified as "right-wing" or members of the "religious right" are considered extremists who may do harm. Ask yourself if you would like to be a parent and have your daughter come home and introduce her boyfriend: "Mom, this is Harry, the right-wing guy I told you about." Or "You are going to like Bill. He is a member of the religious right." You might want to ask why the media so often describes people as right-wing. Less frequently is anyone described as left-wing. Does this mean that many people on the left live in a world in which they view themselves as mainstream? Does it mean that the

media is often liberal and views any other view as extremist? I would be satisfied to just find out how this bird gets off the ground, if it only has one wing.

The ever popular name-calling gambit is used to put down a person or
point of view without resorting to heavy thought. Today the very worst epi-
thet is racist. This word has been known to reduce grown men to a little pud-
dle of liquid. Also popular is the use of words like insensitive, which implies
that you really are racist but the speaker hasn't been able to find the time to
obtain definite proof.

Here the policy question is stated in such a way that you either agree with
the question or you must pin a sign on your chest that says you are "ugly,"
"mean," or "bigot." If you have the inclination, you might want to play a bit
with the words that make politicians and columnists sound eloquent without
being substantive. For example, I recently read the sentence in an opinion
piece, "Americans join the culture of revenge." What if your mother said,
"Johnny, you are on your own; I've decided to join a culture of revenge?"

An example I recently spotted referred to John Bolton, the U.S. ambassa-
dor to the United Nations. A publication described the words in one of
Bolton's speeches as "an extraordinary outburst" against the U.N.[2] One way
to tell if the word usage is legitimate is to ask if you would like someone to
report your words in such a fashion. "Henry made an extraordinary outburst
against his boss." I think not. Outburst seems lacking in courage and nobility.
Can you see Dr. Martin Luther King, Jr., having an "extraordinary outburst"?
Would *The Times* have reported that President Lincoln had an extraordinary
outburst in a speech opening a cemetery at Gettysburg, Pennsylvania?

So what was Bolton's outburst? He was speaking heatedly against a resolution blaming Israel for the deaths of civilians. He said "Many of the spon-
sors of [the] resolution are notorious abusers of human rights themselves, and
were seeking to deflect criticism of their own policies. . . . The Human Rights
Council has quickly fallen into the same trap and delegitimized itself by fo-
cusing attention exclusively on Israel. Meanwhile, it has failed to address real
human rights abuses in Burma, Darfur, the DPKK, and other countries."

Personally I think the man's extraordinary outburst is rather eloquent.

I include the use of slogans in this section because they use seemingly sen-
sible collections of words that really don't carry much information. A politician shouts, "It is time to get this country moving." Well, no one wants a stagnant country, but there isn't much content in the words. Ask: Is there anyone
who could not use this slogan?

Often people try to end the argument by using circular reasoning—words
which contain the assumption that should be proven. For example, if someone asks what we should do about the "homeless crisis," they want you to ac-

cept the premise up front that there is, in fact, a homeless crisis. Perhaps they should have to prove that fact first.

Language has become an important weapon that those who demand political correctness wield effectively. The language of academia and the media always must be most closely watched. Partisans of late have insulted their enemies by calling their own arguments "provocative" or "challenging," while calling the words of opponents "intolerant" or "hateful." I got these particular examples of the misuse of language from an article by David French at frontpagemag.com, "The Unending Hypocrisy of Campus Censorship."[3] French shows how resistant the universities have become to actually practicing freedom of speech on campuses. Through the easy use of phrases such as "McCarthy-like" or "McCarthyism tactics" the left has cowed old-fashioned liberals.

Living in the academic sphere, I've been amused by the cleverness of political activists to subvert freedom of speech by saying that anyone who wishes to speak against them on campus is an enemy of free speech. In late 2007, Columbia University was "provocative" in inviting the president of Iran, Mahmoud Ahmadinejad, to speak on campus so he could once again deny that the Holocaust occurred. The invitation was defended by Columbia's president as a matter of free speech, though the university is notorious for denying a forum to those on the political right.

Political activists employ language to stifle those who challenge their viewpoint or bring a balanced perspective to a public policy discussion. Not many academics and fewer politicians can tolerate charges that their views are "racist" or intolerant of the ideas of others. Even a hint that such an accusation is possible will silence or reign in debate. Language is still a very potent way to control the public realm.[4]

Language even can be a weapon if you don't use any. Since in our time the political left holds sway in much of the media, all they have to do is nothing about covering their opponents. Brilliant books are just ignored instead of reviewed. This works very well. If no one in the media publishes the intelligent questions when they are raised, no one must be bothered to try to answer them. As many a marriage partner has found out, silence is an effective way of shouting disapproval and exerting emotional pressure. In politics a viewpoint given the "silent treatment" is simply marginalized as unimportant. You can't challenge hypocrisy unless the media focus on it.

Silence works especially well when dealing with such topics as the history of the Middle East, about which most people know little. For example the media constantly talks about Israel's "occupation," which begs the question, whose country are they occupying? Once you know the history of the area you know that there hasn't been a country in the areas considered to be occupied (Gaza and the West Bank) from time immemorial. The land was owned mainly by absentee landlords living in Istanbul. It really isn't too clear who owned what in this area. But, if the media will not talk about it, this is hard to point out.

By just using the word *occupation,* which surely sounds like a bad thing, the media can convey the impression that Israel is in the wrong. It turns out the Israel is one of the few countries (perhaps the only one) that can show that it legally purchased much of its land. By not using words like *occupy* to describe post-war foreign policy, you avoid the question, "Hey, isn't that what the U.S. did after World War II in Germany and Japan?"

Another happy device discovered by the left is to state the facts but refuse to draw obvious conclusions from them. *The New York Times* leads the way in this new art form. *The Times* had a three part series warmly supportive of Sheik Reda Shata, who is described as a moderate, kindly man in transition between two worlds.[5] In the story, he is described as a member of the Islamic Society of Bay Ridge, which has frequently been a center of militant Islam and defense for terrorists. A sermon at the Bay Ridge Mosque was cited as inspiration when Rashid Baz murdered a rabbinical student. Sheik Shata praised a woman suicide bomber as a "martyr." This man warrants sympathetic portrayal as a moderate?

On Sunday, June 4, 2006, *The Times* told the story of Canadians who were advancing in carrying out a plot to blow up buildings and cut off the head of Canada's prime minister without once mentioning that the religion of all of the plotters happened to be Islam. The closest *The Times* came to making this connection was to say that the "17 men were mainly of South Asian descent." *The Times* used the word *Muslim* once in the first thirty-five paragraphs. Tarek Fatah, the communications director of the Muslim Canadian Congress, was quoted as saying that one of the suspects is a "well-known and fiery figure in the Toronto area's South Asian community."

Since the attack on September 11, 2001, *The Times* has seemed frequently to go to extreme lengths to protect the honor of Islam. Numerous features have pointed out the positive aspects of North American Muslims and the religion as a whole. The impression is that Muslims throughout the world have suffered because of the actions by a few extremists and that this is the suffering we should focus on. These are aberrations in what is, after all, according *The Times,* a most peaceful religion. There is truth in such a description of Islam, but it certainly is superficial and one-dimensional. For example, the term *peace* in Islamic theology is no easy idea to define. Do the military conquests by Islam in the Middle East, North Africa, Eastern Europe, Spain, and parts of Italy, and France fit the Islamic idea of a peace movement? Depending on the particular group doing the defining, peace can cover acts that seem un-peaceful to others. Likewise, The Times avoids using the word terrorist in the same sentence as Muslim or Islam, lest anyone associate Islam with terrorism.

A conceit that approaches arrogance is hard to miss in this kind of journalism. *The New York Times* doesn't think people will realize that the editorial policy being followed has a bias. Any casual reader knows that *The Times* does not hesitate to tell the religious affiliation of perpetrators of violence who are Jews or Christians. By transparently manipulating language, the reporters seem to assume that intelligent readers will believe that the plotters in Canada were motivated by their South Asian ethnicity.

I am being hard on one influential newspaper, but *The Times* is only contributing to a trend. Others also left out key information regarding that terror plot. Reaction to the plot in Canada especially indicated that the elite seem to think that the non-elite citizens lack the capacity to think at all. A Royal Canadian Mounted Police Officer used the phrase "broad strata" to describe the origins of the plotters they had arrested. The Toronto chief of police divined that these folks were not motivated by "faith." The Toronto Star, in its story, said that "it is difficult to find a common denominator" among the group.

Sometimes your enemies help. Such is the case with language used by the European Commission, according to a Reuters press report on April 16, 2006. This international consultation commission employs twenty "terminologists" to insure that members of the European Union use politically correct language. They have been on the hunt for a "non-emotive lexicon for discussing radicalism." They say "certainly 'Islamic terrorism' is something we will not use. . . . We talk about 'terrorists who abusively invoke Islam." According to the Reuters press report, "The aim of the guidelines is to avoid the use of words that could unnecessarily offend Muslims and spark radicalization."[6]

The EU commissioners said that *Jihad* was under review. "Jihad means something for you and me, it means something else for a Muslim," one member of the commission said. "Jihad is a perfectly positive concept of trying to fight evil within yourself." Jihad does have meanings that extend beyond benign self-searching. That Jihad is the spiritual equivalent of flossing regularly may come as a surprise to the many centuries of infidels who have been subjugated by Moslems, as well as those who keep up with the news today.

Chapter Twelve

Inputs or Outputs?

During election campaigns, often a candidate will signal concern by saying that if he or she is elected more money will be spent on . . . (fill in the blank depending on what voter bloc is being addressed). I have nothing against spending more money. I have had very few problems that were made worse by spending more money. However, should you count how much money is being spent on education, or should you ask how much education is really taking place?

The most visible input is money, which should buy a desired output. I have nothing against spending more money. But if we are putting money into a worthy project, we should be looking at how much output we are buying. We have looked at education financing and suggested that all the financing in the world won't necessarily help educational programs teach better. Should you count how much money is being spent on education, or should you ask how much educating is taking place for the money already spent?

It is easier to win an argument if we don't have to show results, while our opponents do. For example, perhaps an incumbent's record of success in the sphere of education has not been stellar. The opponent points the finger, de-crying a lack of results. The candidate then promises to spend more money on education. The incumbent has to show tangible results, the challenger simply has to promise more. All of those who will receive that money will sure be happy. All of the parents who want their children to do better in school will be happier, at least for the moment.

But what if I am a challenger who knows from bitter experience that more money will not guarantee better results given the situation in these schools? What should I do? Should I say that we should look at results? What can I promise? What if I have looked at the actual research and I have discovered that, while more money rarely hurts, the key determinants of educational results come from the influence of the family and the peer group? What can I promise to do, change parents if they don't emphasize the worth of education? Can I promise to throw out poor peer groups? How would I do that?

If I actually care about the truth, I might say that I will try new methods of teaching or demand higher standards of effort from the students. Meanwhile, my opponent is out there saying that he will fix everything by spending more money. Would you vote for the guy promising cash on the barrelhead or the guy who needs seven paragraphs to explain what he will do and doesn't mention the words cash or barrelhead?

It takes a strong citizen to resist those who campaign by promising inputs as opposed to those who promise outputs. Spending more money is a lot easier to promise and produce than results, especially in the most important areas like education.

Think of inputs and outputs in terms of cost and benefit. This can get quite messy when the subject is health care resources. Policies under debate here are about allocating health resources when that could determine who lives and who dies. How much input in resources should be put into the output of lives saved. David Stipp reported in the *Wall Street Journal* on a massive study of cost efficiency in medicine by the Center for Risk Analysis, Harvard University School of Public Health.[1]

The *Wall Street Journal* asked, "Which saves lives more cheaply, heart transplants or curing industrial pollution to prevent cancer?"[2] It is a more complicated question than might be at first imagined. One can only estimate how many people would have gotten sick and died that will not because of a pollution reduction program that may cost $2.5 million. A heart transplant has obvious direct results for one person at half the cost. But would the input money be better allocated for an indirect benefit for many than for the direct benefit of a single heart patient who lives a few more years.

We could save a lot more lives by reallocating funds. Some things we do to save lives are incredibly costly, and others are happily quite cheap. But if you said anything like this or acted on this information, you would be ripped apart as heartless. According to the Harvard study, it costs very little to save a life by immunization and prenatal care. Enough flu shots to save a life cost $600 (in 1994). To save a life by home radon controls cost $141,000. Removing asbestos cost $900,000 per life saved. Radiation controls saved a life for every $7.4 million spent.[3]

Input-output cost-benefit analysis has been studied in medical research for years, but its influence on public policy has been relatively small. Using such methods to run a government program just seems too heartless.

Answers to What Everybody "Knows"

1. Between 2001 and 2003, 51,025 people in the U.S. died of diseases caused by the HIV-AIDS virus. Source: Center for Disease Control (CDC) mortality data. During the same time period, 3.078 million people in the U.S. died of cancer. Source: American Cancer Society. During this period 7 million (worldwide; 2.07 million in the U.S.) died of coronary heart disease. Source: American Heart Association.
2. Each year, about 150 U.S. police officers are killed in the line of duty. Recent statistics: 2002, 157; 2003, 147; 2004, 162; 2005, 157; 2006, 145. Source: Federal Bureau of Investigation crime statistics.
3. In September 2006, 1,384,960 people were on active duty in the regular U.S. Army, Navy, Marines, Air Force and Coast Guard, not including reserve units. Source: U.S. Department of Defense.
4. Israel is thinking of giving up the land known as the West Bank so that the Palestinians can have their own nation. If Israel gives this land, the nation would be nine miles wide at its "waist," the narrowest width of the country, which extends inland from the Mediterranean Sea at a point north of Tel Aviv.
5. If the federal government confiscated all the income of taxpayers who make $1 million a year and used this money to run the federal government, the nation would have enough revenue for seventeen days of expenditures. Source: 2007 Statistical Abstract.
6. In 1989, after tests on mice produced tumors, the U.S. banned use of the chemical Alar, which was used to keep apples from rotting prior to harvest. To reach the level of exposure that caused tumors in mice, a child would have to drink nineteen thousand quarts of apple juice. Source: Environmental Protection Agency Science Advisory Panel.

7. According to the best documented and most comprehensive study on school performance, family and peer group are the two most important factors determine academic success?

8. In 1961, Saudi Arabia outlawed slavery. In 1981, Mauritania banned slavery. Mauritania still has not gone so far as to "outlaw" the practice, assessing criminal penalties. Source: Pascal Fletcher, "Mauritania candidates promise to outlaw slavery," Reuters News Service, March 2007.

9. The world's five most deadly diseases are: (1) heart disease; (2) vascular disease, e.g., stroke; (3) respiratory disease, e.g., tuberculosis; (4) HIV/AIDS virus; (5) pulmonary disease, e.g., emphysema. Source: United Nations World Health Organization report, "The World's Deadliest Diseases."

10. During World War II, an estimated 20 million people were killed by the military forces of the Empire of Japan; approximately 2.5 million Japanese lost their lives as a result of the war. Source: R. J. Rummel. Statistics of Democide: Genocide and Mass Murder since 1900 (1998).

11. The range of per capita household income in the U.S. by racial group, highest to lowest, is (1) Asian; (2) white; (3) Hispanic; (4) black. Source: U.S. Census Bureau.

12. The average 2007 expenditure per pupil in New Jersey is $12,098 (a 3.1 percent increase over 2006. Source: New Jersey Department of Education. New Jersey students ranked thirty-seventh among U.S. high school students in Scholastic Aptitude Test scores. Source: College Board Association.

13. The U.S. federal government of the United States in 2005 spent an average $10.573 billion each day?$440.5 million an hour. Source: U.S. Census Bureau.

14. The U.S. federal income tax burden paid by the wealthiest 1 percent of taxpayers is 28 percent of federal tax revenues. The tax burden paid by the lower half of income earners is 15 percent (taxpayers earning less than $50,000 a year). Source: 2007 *Statistical Abstract.*

15. Cities, highways, railroads, airports, and other development use 3.6 percent of the total U.S. land mass. Source: U.S. Department of Agriculture Natural Resources Inventory.

16. The average American still produces about four pounds of solid waste per day, about the same as in 1900. Source: Environmental Protection Agency.

17. False. The average household in Mexico City produces one-third more garbage a day than the average household in the United States. Source: John Tierney, "Recycling is Garbage," *The New York Times*, June 30, 1996.

18. True. If all of the solid waste produced in the United States during the past century was placed in a landfill, that landfill would require less than 100 square miles. Source: "Fun with Statistics: Garbage Edition," Evolving Excellence Web site, evolvingexcellence.com.
19. Some 87 percent of all the paper used in the U.S. is produced from trees that are planted and grown for the apple industry.
20. Medical grants for research into causes, cures, and prevention of leading causes of death amount to: $900 for each lung cancer death; $3,500 for each prostate cancer death; $9,000 for each breast cancer death; and $34,000 for each HIV-AIDS related death. Source: American Cancer Society.
21. The ten most dangerous jobs in the U.S. in terms of the number of deaths and injuries per capita of the work force are: (1) commercial fishing; (2) logging; (3) piloting aircraft; (4) structural metal work; (5) refuse/recyclable material collection; (6) farming/ranching; (7) electric line installation and repair; (8) over-the-road freight hauling; (9) all agriculture work; (10) construction. Source: Les Christie, "America's Most Dangerous Jobs," *CNN Money,* October 13, 2003.

Notes

CHAPTER 1. FACTS

1. Steven D. Levitt and Stephen J. Dubner, *Freakonomics: A Rogue Economist Explores the Hidden Side of Everything* (New York: William Morrow, 2005), 90.

2. Ibid. See also Kenneth J. Beirne, "America's Homeless: A Manageable Problem and Solution," Backgrounder Update 44, Devos Center for Religion and Civil Society. See on the Heritage Foundation Web site at heritage.org/Research/Religion/bu44. A wealth of information on homelessness is available through the "knowledge base" of the Homelessness Resource Center, nrchmi.samhsa.gov/Browse.

3. Thomas Sowell, "Lying Statistics," *Jewish World Review,* June 28, 2001, at jewishworldreview.com.

4. *USA Today,* March 7, 2006.

5. Welfare statistics from *The World Almanac and Book of Facts, 2007* (New York: World Almanac, 2007). While much of the information used in this volume can be gained in other almanac's, the *World Almanac* is the author's almanac of choice and will be used throughout.

6. *Annual Social and Economic Supplement,* 2006 (2005 data). See on the U.S. Census Bureau Web site at census.gov/hhes/www/poverty/detailedpovtabs.

7. The U.S. Census Bureau has a wealth of demographic information in easy reach. Some of this data came from the historical poverty tables for people at census .gov/hhes/www/poverty/histpov/perindex and families at census.gov/hhes/www/poverty/histpov/famindex.

8. Terence P. Jeffrey, "Best Poverty Predictor: Family Status, Not Race," *Human Events,* September 26, 2005.

9. See aspe.hhs.gov/poverty.

10. Martin Gross, *The Government Racket: Washington Waste from A to Z* (New York: Avon, 2000).

11. United Nations World Health Organization, *World Health Report,* 2004. See at who.int/features/qa/18/en/index.

12. One clearinghouse for scientific data and activism to return to the use of DDT around the world can be found through the African American Environmental Association. Their Web site at aaenvironment.com/DDT includes links to petitions signed by scientists and medical community leaders.

13. Sandi Doughton, "Taking on Third World Water," Seattle, Wash., *Times,* September 9, 2006. See at seattletimes.nwsource.com/cgi-bin/PrintStory.pl?document_id=2003469254&zsection_id=2002111777&slug=cleanwater09m&date=20061209. Most programs are now "point-of-use" chlorination efforts in the home, but these programs may be too expensive for most in the developing world See a report by epidemiologists Benjamin F. Arnold and John M. Colford, Jr., in the American Journal of Tropical Medicine and Hygiene at ajtmh.org/cgi/content/abstract/76/2/354.

14. Nigel Bruce, Rogelio Perez-Padilla, and Rachel Albalak, "Indoor air pollution in developing countries: a major environmental and public health challenge," *World Health Organization Bulletin,* 2000: 1078–92. See at who.int/docstore/bulletin/pdf/2000/issue9/bul0711.

15. At this writing, the latest edition, The Statistical Abstract of the United States, 2007, is available online at the U.S. Census Bureau Web site at census.gov/prod/www/statistical-abstract.

16. "Homelessness: Programs and the People They Serve," a summary of studies for the U.S. Department of Housing and Urban Development, 1999. The landmark study of homelessness is the 1996 National Survey of Homeless Assistance Providers and Clients. A Los Angeles National Institute on Drug Abuse study in 1997 found that 71 percent of homeless adolescents abused drugs. June Wyman, "Drug Abuse Among Runaway and Homeless Youths Calls for Focused Outreach Solutions," NIDA Notes, 12.3 (May-June 1997).

17. David U. Himmelstein, et al., "MarketWatch: Illness And Injury As Contributors To Bankruptcy," *Health Affairs,* February 2, 2005: 10.

18. Statistical Abstract 2007. I find raw numbers in table 673, "Money Income of Households—Distribution by Income Level and Selected Characteristics: 2004." See also Table 692, "People Below Poverty Level and Below 125 Percent of Poverty Level by Race and Hispanic Origin: 1980 to 2004," and table 678, "Money Income of Families—Percent Distribution by Income Level in Constant (2003) Dollars: 1980 to 2003."

19. The 2005 statistics, published in October 2007, can be seen at Gerald Prante, "Summary of Latest Federal Individual Income Tax Data," Fiscal Facts, 104. The online Tax Foundation newsletter can be seen at taxfoundation.org/files/ff104.

20. Washington, D.C.: Cato Institute, 2000.

21. See, for example, the results of several studies on the media at mediaresearch.org/biasbasics.

22. Fourth ed., New York: American Council on Science and Health, 2004.

23. Ibid.

24. Ibid.

25. Denise Venable, "The Wage Gap Myth," Analysis Paper 392 (April 12, 2002), National Center for Policy Analysis.

26. Jane Waldfogel and Susan E. Mayer, "Male-Female Differences in the Low-Wage Labor Market," JCPR Working Paper 70 (Chicago: Joint Center for Poverty Research).

27. Eduardo Porter, "The Search for Illegal Immigrants Stops at the Workplace," *The New York Times,* March 5, 2006, BU3.

28. Ibid.

29. To date, there have been problems with the program for the new system. To be fair, the current Immigration and Naturalization Service database is both unwieldy and inaccurate. It is also unknown. Those who train employers in background checks seldom even mention it. The INS database on deportables is not available for private reference. Under the Bipartisan Immigration Reform Bill of 2007, this database would be overhauled into a database on 150 million workers, called EEVS or the Employee Eligibility Verification System. At this writing, there are some questions about whether the EEVS will be constitutional on privacy grounds.

30. *The New York Times,* March 26, 2006. Available online at 64.233.167.104/ search?q=cache:-a-_F6EsinkJ:www.investorsfordirectoraccountability.org/ documents/GretchenMorgenson.pdf+Fund+Manager,+Time+Pick+Side&hl=en&ct= clnk&cd=2&gl=us.

31. The Institute estimates that corporate subsidies will top $100 billion in 2008. See Ralph Deeds, "The Corporate Welfare Congress," on the Cato Institute Web site at hubpages.com/hub/The-Corporate-Welfare-Congress.

32. Joseph DiPardo, "Outlook for Biomass Ethanol Production and Demand," Energy Information Administration Analysis Paper, available online at ethanol-gec.org/ information/briefing/6.

33. Michelle Malkin, "Who Let Malvo Loose?" *Jewish World Review,* October 25, 2002. See online at jewishworldreview.com/michelle/malkin102502.

34. "Homeowner Shoots, Kills Intruder in Aldine," *Chronicle,* December 21, 2004.

CHAPTER 2. COMPARATIVE ANALYSIS

1. United Nations Statistics Division, 2005; *The New York Times,* October 18, 2006.

2. Newark, N.J., *Star-Ledger.*

3. Deborah Lynn Guber, "Getting What You Pay for: The Debate over Equity in Public School Expenditures," *Journal of Statistics Education,* 7.2 (1999). Available online at amstat.org/publications/jse/secure/v7n2/datasets.guber.

4. Mark Berkey Gerard, "The Real Issues in the 2005 Mayoral Race," *Gotham Gazette,* October 17, 2005.

5. A good analysis of the New Jersey situation is found in "School Funding" on the League of Women Voters of New Jersey Web site at lwvnj.org/action/2000/edfunding.

6. A handy database for checking the health of New Jersey's respective systems is available through Asbury Park Press at php.app.com/sat06web/search.

7. Travel advisories for all countries where there are crime concerns are available on the U.S. Department of State Web site at travel.state.gov/travel/cis_pa_tw/cis_pa_ tw_1168.

8. The very title of the "universal health care" debate in the U.S. indicates the inexact way language is used. It isn't that supporters of universal health care do not say they are talking about insurance, but they frequently fuzz the distinction between health insurance and health care. One interesting example of this, ironically from the medical community supporters of universal care is found on the American Medical Student Association for October 30, 2007, at amsa.org/uhc/.

9. This is an annual book and is available online with an acrobat reader program at cdc.gov/nchs/hus.

10. Nathan Schumukler and Edward Marcus, eds., *Inflation through the Ages: Economic, Social, Psychological and Historical Aspects* (New York: Columbia University Press, 1983).

CHAPTER 3. OPPOSING VIEWS

1. *The New York Times,* April 8, 2001, A1.

2. A good general explanation of the Accountability Project's origin and roots is John S. James, "AIDS Service Organizations: Accountability Issue Surfaces in San Francisco," *The Body,* November 7, 1997, at thebody.com/content/art31516. See Petrelis's blog, "The Petrelis Files," at mpetrelis.blogspot.com.

3. "Report Criticizes Salaries of Top AIDS Execs," *The Data Lounge,* May 7, 1998, at datalounge.com/cgi-bin/iowa/english/newsarchive/article/3011.

4. New York: Bantam, 2000.

5. A26.

6. "Study of Doctors Sees Little Effect of Affirmative Action on Careers," *The New York Times,* October 8, 1997, A1.

7. Ibid.

8. Washington, D.C.: Regnery, 2004.

9. Ibid.

10. Paul Cassell, "We're Not Executing the Innocent," *Wall Street Journal,* June 16, 2000, A14.

11. Ibid.

12. Gabriel Rotello, "AIDS is Still an Exceptional Disease," *The New York Times,* August 22, 1997.

13. Newark, New Jersey, *Star-Ledger,* November 1997, 24.

14. December 15, 2005. See this article at nytimes.com/2005/12/15/books/15masl. Maslin is reviewing a book by Aaron J. Klein, *Striking Back: The 1972 Munich Olympics Massacre and Israel's Deadly Response* (New York: Random House, 2005).

15. Edward Rothstein, *The New York Times,* December 26, 2005. See at nytimes.com/2005/12/26/arts/26conn.

16. Ibid.

17. "The Keepers of K Street," *Wall Street Journal,* January 17, 2006, A16.

18. Nobelprize.org, at nobelprize.org/nobel_prizes/peace/laureates/1970/borlaug-bio.

19. Nobelprize.org at nobelprize.org/nobel_prizes/medicine/laureates/1977/yalow-autobio.

CHAPTER 5. THE NUMBERS

1. U.S. Census Bureau, "Health Insurance Coverage, 2004." See at census.gov/hhes/www/hlthins/hlthin04/hlth04asc.

2. "The 2005 HHS Poverty Guidelines," U.S. Department of Health and Human Services. See at aspe.hhs.gov/poverty/05poverty.

3. "Cougar Hardened Engineer Vehicle [HEV)" at Global Security.org, global security.org/military/systems/ground/cougar-hev.

4. "Buffalo and Cougar," Group, Inc.: Force Protection, Inc., at gichd.org/fileadmin/pdf/publications/MDE_Catalogue_2006/MDE_Cat_2006_Section_7.

5. "F-22 Raptor: FY 2006 Procurement & Events," *Defense Industry Daily,* September 30, 2006. See at defenseindustrydaily.com/f22-raptor-fy-2006-procurement-events-updated-02212.

6. *Wall Street Journal,* October 15, 1999, A1.

7. "The Carriers, The List," United States Navy, chinfo.navy.mil/navpalib/ships/carriers/cv-list1. "CVN 21 / CVN-X / CVX: History," Global Security.org. See at global security.org/military/systems/ship/cvx-history. Britain and France are planning to jointly build three aircraft carriers, to be delivered between 2012 and 2014.

8. Noah Shachtman, "Defending America," *Popular Mechanics,* April 2006.

9. Thomas Sowell, "Lying Statistics," *Jewish World Review,* June 28, 2001. See at jewishworldreview.com.

10. Ibid.

11. "Former Police Officers Being Sued By Los Angeles Police Department," Lawcore.com, November 22, 2006. See at lawcore.com/legal-information/03-22-06.

12. See kaisernetwork.org/daily_reports/rep_index.cfm?DR_ID=42518.

13. See, e.g., kff.org/medicare/upload/1066-09; therubins.com/medicare/drugcostIIa.

14. Gerald Plante, *Fiscal Facts.* See the Tax Foundation newsletter at taxfoundation.org/news/show/1916.

CHAPTER 6. HISTORY

1. Robert Rector, "The Fiscal Cost of Low-Skill Workers to the American Taxpayer," testimony before the Subcommittee on Immigration, Committee on the Judiciary, U.S. House of Representatives, May 1, 2007. See at judiciary.house.gov/media/pdfs/Rector070501.

2. Stephen Moore, *It's Getting Better All the Time: 100 Greatest Trends of the Last 100 Years* (Washington, D.C.: Cato Institute, 2000).

3. New York: Random House, 1962.

4. Julian Simon, *The Ultimate Resource 2: People, Materials, Environment* (Princeton, N.J.: Princeton University Press, 1998).

5. Ibid.

6. Thomas Sowell, *Ethnic America: A History* (New York: Basic: 1981).

7. Susanne Everett, *The Slaves: an Illustrated History of the Monstrous Evil* (New York, Putnam's Sons, 1978).

8. Richard Pipes, *Property and Freedom* (New York: Vintage, 2000).

9. Lawrence H. Keeley, *War before Civilization: the Myth of the Peaceful Savage* (New York: Oxford University Press USA, 1996).

10. Joshua Muravchik, *Heaven on Earth: The Rise and Fall of Socialism, a history of socialist fantasies* (Lanham, Md.: Encounter, 2002); Alastair Hamilton, *The Appeal of Fascism: A Study of Intellectuals and Fascism, 1919–1945* (New York: MacMillan, 1971).

11. Eugene Lyons, *The Red Decade: the Stalinist Penetration of America* (Indianapolis: Bobbs-Merrill, 1941).

12. Ibid.

13. Richard Wolin, *The Seduction of Unreason: The Intellectual Romance with Fascism from Nietzsche to Postmodernism* (Princeton, N.J.: Princeton University Press, 2004); Stéphane Courtois, ed., *The Black Book of Communism: Crimes, Terror, and Repression* (1997; ET, Cambridge, Mass.: Harvard University Press, 1999); Paul Hollander, *Political Pilgrims: Travels of Western Intellectuals to the Soviet Union, China, and Cuba* (reprint ed., Piscataway, N.J.: Transaction, 1983); or Raymond Aron, *The Opium of the Intellectuals* (Piscataway, N.J.: Transaction, 2001).

14. Niall Ferguson, *Colossus: The Rise and Fall of the American Empire* (New York: Penguin, 2004).

15. T. R. Fehrenbach, *This Kind of War: The Classic Korean War History* (1951; reprint ed., Dulles, Va.: Potomac, 2001).

16. Frank Ryan, *The Forgotten Plague: How the Battle Against Tuberculosis Was Won—and Lost* (Boston: Back Bay, 1994)

17. Victor Davis Hanson, *An Autumn of War: What America Learned from September 11 and the War on Terrorism* (New York: Random House, 2002).

18. Fehrenbach, *This Kind of War.*

19. Robert Leckie, *Strong Men Armed* (Cambridge, Mass.: Da Capo, 1997).

20. W. Thomas Smith, "The Great Christmas Night Raid," Townhall.com, December 22, 2006, at townhall.com/columnists/column.aspx?UrlTitle=the_great_christmas_night_raid&ns=WThomasSmithJr&dt=12/22/2006&page=full&comments=true.

CHAPTER 7. DOUBLE STANDARD

1. An overview of the story of Kinneret Boosany can be found at shirleybarenholz.com/PP/NP/KIN/KINS.

2. *The New York Times,* January 19, 1997.
3. New York: Dover PBK, 1980.

CHAPTER 8. THE MEDIA

1. Ben Shapiro, *Brainwashed: How Universities Indoctrinate America's Youth* (Nashville: Thomas Nelson, 2004).
2. Leslie Eaton, "Study Sees Increase in Illegal Spanish Workers in New Orleans," *The New York Times,* June 8, 2006, 16.
3. Ibid.
4. For a view of the views surrounding Stanley "Tookie" Williams's execution, see Jennifer Warren and Maura Dolan, "Tookie Williams is Executed," *Los Angeles Times,* December 13, 2005.
5. Most Web sites relating to the victims of Williams and the support for his cause are no longer functioning. Savetookie.org and tookie.com sites are still in operation with books for sale and the story of his nomination for a Nobel Peace Prize by a Notre Dame de Namur University philosophy professor.
6. Eric Dash, "Off to the Races Again, Leaving Many Behind," *The New York Times,* April 9, 2006. See at nytimes.com/2006/04/09/business/businessspecial/09pay.
7. Ibid.
8. Ibid.

CHAPTER 9. SOLUTIONS OR TRADE-OFFS?

1. "Hurricane Spending and the Federal Budget," Joint Economic Committee Research Report 109-29, February 2006. See at house.gov/jec/publications/109/rr109-29.
2. Valerie Bauerlein, "On Topsail Island, Storms Fuel Battle over Right to Build," Realestatejournal.com, online publication of the *Wall Street Journal,* December 8, 2005. See at realestatejournal.com/buysell/regionalnews/20051208-bauerlein.
3. Gordon Clark, "Ceasing production and sales of surfboard blanks," *Surfer* Magazine, surfermag.com/features/onlineexclusives/clarkfoamletter/.
4. Gina Kolata, "Exchanging Cigarettes for Bagels," *The New York Times,* December 19, 2004. See at nytimes.com/2004/12/19/weekinreview/19kola.

CHAPTER 10. APPLES AND ORANGES

Associated Press, "Report details black-white wealth inequality: Urban League study finds nagging gaps in net worth, health care," MSNBC, April 5, 2005. See at msnbc.msn.com/id/7397962

CHAPTER 11. LANGUAGE

1. November 20, 2000.
2. November 19, 2006.
3. February 28, 2006.
4. *Columbia News,* Public Affairs Office, Columbia University, September 24, 2007.
5. Andrea Elliott, "An Imam in America," March 5–7, 2006.
6. "Translating the Truth into European Muslim-Speak," Planck's Constant Web site, at plancksconstant.org/blog1/2006/04/translating_the_truth_into_eur.

CHAPTER 12. INPUTS OR OUTPUTS?

1. David Stipp, "Prevention May be Costlier than a Cure," *Wall Street Journal,* July 6, 1994.
2. Ibid.
3. Ibid.